new interchange

English for international communication

Jack C. Richards

with Jonathan Hull and Susan Proctor

workbook

3

New Interchange Workbook
revision prepared by Jonathan Hull.

CAMBRIDGE
UNIVERSITY PRESS

PUBLISHED BY THE PRESS SYNDICATE OF THE UNIVERSITY OF CAMBRIDGE
The Pitt Building, Trumpington Street, Cambridge, United Kingdom

CAMBRIDGE UNIVERSITY PRESS
The Edinburgh Building, Cambridge CB2 2RU, UK
40 West 20th Street, New York, NY 10011–4211, USA
10 Stamford Road, Oakleigh, VIC 3166, Australia
Ruiz de Alarcón 13, 28014 Madrid, Spain
Dock House, The Waterfront, Cape Town 8001, South Africa

http://www.cambridge.org

First published 1998
7th printing 2000

New Interchange Workbook 3 has been developed from *Interchange* Workbook 3,
first published by Cambridge University Press in 1991.

Printed in the United Kingdom at the University Press, Cambridge

Typeface New Century Schoolbook   *System* QuarkXPress®   [AH]

A catalog record for this book is available from the British Library

ISBN 0 521 62844 X Student's Book 3
ISBN 0 521 62843 1 Student's Book 3A
ISBN 0 521 62842 3 Student's Book 3B
ISBN 0 521 62841 5 Workbook 3
ISBN 0 521 62840 7 Workbook 3A
ISBN 0 521 62839 3 Workbook 3B
ISBN 0 521 62838 5 Teacher's Edition 3
ISBN 0 521 62837 7 Teacher's Manual 3
ISBN 0 521 62836 9 Class Audio Cassettes 3
ISBN 0 521 62834 2 Student's Audio Cassette 3A
ISBN 0 521 62832 6 Student's Audio Cassette 3B
ISBN 0 521 62835 0 Class Audio CDs 3
ISBN 0 521 62833 4 Student's Audio CD 3A
ISBN 0 521 62831 8 Student's Audio CD 3B
ISBN 0 521 95019 8 Audio Sampler 1–3

Forthcoming
ISBN 0 521 62882 2 Placement Test (revised)
ISBN 0 521 77377 6 Lab Guide 3
ISBN 0 521 77376 8 Lab Cassettes 3

Available from the First Edition
ISBN 0 521 46759 4 Placement Test
ISBN 0 521 42222 1 Lab Guide 3
ISBN 0 521 42221 3 Lab Cassettes 3

Book design, art direction, and layout services: Adventure House, NYC
Illustrators: Adventure House, Randy Jones, Mark Kaufman, Kevin Spaulding, Sam Viviano
Photo researchers: Sylvia P. Bloch, Joan Scafarello

Contents

Acknowledgments

TEXT CREDITS

The authors and publishers are grateful for permission to reproduce the following material. Every endeavor has been made to contact copyright owners, and apologies are expressed for omissions.

3 From Barry Fantoni, "Heights of Fashion," *Weekend Guardian*, 21–22, July 1990. Reprinted by permission.

39 Greenpeace Campaign Report #27, June 1997, Canonbury Villas, London, UK.

45 Copyright © 1990 by David Guterson. Originally appeared in *Harper's Magazine*.

52 From Graham Ball, "Feng Shui reaches the DIY superstore," *The Independent Sunday*. Reprinted by permission.

94 Used with permission of Médecins Sans Frontières, from *Dispatches: MSF UK*, 124–132, Summer 1997.

ILLUSTRATORS

Randy Jones 1, 4, 6, 7, 10, 16, 18, 20, 25, 28, 29, 33, 44, 50, 51, 64, 65, 66, 69, 73, 78, 85, 88, 96

Mark Kaufman 17, 31, 34, 54

Kevin Spaulding 5, 13 (*bottom*), 84

Sam Viviano 2, 8, 13 (*top*), 14, 15, 22, 23, 27, 30, 40, 53, 59, 61, 62, 76, 77, 86, 87, 92

PHOTOGRAPHIC CREDITS

The authors and publishers are grateful for permission to reproduce the following photographs. Every endeavor has been made to contact copyright owners, and apologies are expressed for omissions.

9 (*top row, left to right*) © Peter Langone/International Stock Photography; © Robert Phillips/The Image Bank; © Morris Lane/The Stock Market; (*bottom row, left to right*) © Nancy D'Antonio/Photo Researchers; © Michael Nelson/FPG; © Patti & Milt Putnam/The Stock Market

12 (*top row, left to right*) © Joe Cornish/Tony Stone Images; © Jeff Zaruba/The Stock Market; (*bottom row, left to right*) © Peter Steiner/The Stock Market; © Peter Beck/The Stock Market

19 (*top*) © Telegraph Colour Library/FPG; (*bottom*) © M.P. Kahl/Photo Researchers

21 © Robert Ketchum

24 (*from left to right*) © Michael Paras/International Stock Photography; © Jose L. Pelaez/The Stock Market; © James Davis/International Stock Photography; © Dan Bosler/Tony Stone Images; © Dan Bosler/Tony Stone Images

26 © Sovfoto/Eastfoto

32 (*left*) © Steven Peters/Tony Stone Images; (*right*) © Jackson Smith/Uniphoto

38 © William B. Folsom/Uniphoto

39 Courtesy of Greenpeace, USA

41 (*top*) © Richard Laird/FPG; (*bottom*) © Max Hilaire/The Image Bank

45 © James Davis/International Stock Photography

46 (*left to right*) © Ron Chapple/FPG; © Michael Philip Manheim/International Stock Photography; © Jon Feingersh/The Stock Market

47 (*top row, left to right*) © Don Smetzer/Tony Stone Images; © Scott Barrow/International Stock Photography; (*bottom row, left to right*) © Amwell/Tony Stone Images; © Robert E. Daemmrich/Tony Stone Images

48 (*left*) © Ursula Markus/Photo Researchers; (*right*) © Robert A. Isaacs/Photo Researchers

49 (*top to bottom*) © Michael Hayman/Photo Researchers; © Jeff Greenberg/Photo Researchers; © Chuck Savage/The Stock Market

52 Photograph © Bridget Morley from page 139 of *The Personal Feng Shui Manual* (1998), by permission of Gaia Books Ltd., London.

55 (*top*) © Archive Photos/Frank Driggs Collection; (*bottom*) © Tom Stoddart/Katz/Woodfin Camp & Associates

56 (*top*) © Archive Photos; (*bottom*) © Sally Weiner Grotto/The Stock Market

57 © Dr. A.C. Twomey/Photo Researchers

58 (*top*) © David Hardy/Science Photo Library/Photo Researchers; (*bottom*) © Ed Wheeler/The Stock Market

60 (*top*) © Jose Pelaez Photography/The Stock Market; (*bottom*) © Phil Jason/Tony Stone Images

63 (*left*) © AP/Wide World Photos; (*right*) © Georges Merillon/Gamma Liaison

67 © Jay Freis/The Image Bank

68 © Mugshots/The Stock Market

71 (*top left*) Advertisement used with permission from Ford. (*right*) Advertisement used with permission from Kraft Foods. (*bottom left*) Advertisement used with permission from the American Automobile Association.

72 Advertisement used with permission from Benetton.

74 (*top left*) © Harald Sund/The Image Bank; (*center right*) © Corbis-Bettmann; (*bottom left*) © Jean-Marc Giboux/Gamma Liaison

75 © Robert Hutchinson/Gamma Liaison; (*insert*) © Corbis-Bettmann

79 (*left*) © Lynn Goldsmith/Corbis; (*right*) © Christopher Weil/Corbis

80 (*left*) © Paul Howell/Gamma Liaison; (*all others*) © Gooseberry Farms, Westport, MA

81 © The Jim Henson Company

82 (*left*) © J. Blaustein/Woodfin Camp & Associates; (*right*) © Fotos International/Archive Photos

83 © AP/Wide World Photos

89 © Jim Hodson/FSP/Gamma Liaison

90 © Jay Freis/The Image Bank

93 (*left*) © Mugshots/The Stock Market; (*right*) © John Olson/The Stock Market

94 © Tine Dhoore/Courtesy Médecins Sans Frontières

95 © Martha Cooper/The Viesti Collection

That's what friends are for!

1 Complete these descriptions with the words from the list.

1. The new secretary is pretty _____high-strung_____ .
   He's really nervous and gets easily upset.

2. The Chans like meeting new people and having friends over for dinner.
   They're one of the most _____ couples I know.

3. You can't trust Jane. She always promises to do something, and then
   she never does it. She's pretty _____ .

4. John is so _____ ! He always thinks his own ideas
   are right and never listens to what other people say.

5. Tina seems to think she's the most important person in the whole
   world! She's really _____ .

☐ egotistical
☑ high-strung
☐ opinionated
☐ sociable
☐ unreliable

2 Opposites

A Complete the chart by forming the opposites of the adjectives in the list.
Use *in-* and *un-*. Then check your answers in a dictionary.

☑ ambitious   ☐ dependent   ☐ formal   ☐ reliable
☐ attractive   ☐ direct   ☐ popular   ☐ sensitive
☑ competent   ☐ experienced   ☐ reasonable   ☐ sociable

incompetent

Opposites with *in-*		Opposites with *un-*	
incompetent	_____	unambitious	_____
_____	_____	_____	_____
_____	_____	_____	_____

B Write four sentences using any of the words in part A.

Example: _Fred is very ambitious at work, but he's inexperienced. He still has a lot to learn._

1. _____
2. _____
3. _____
4. _____

3 *Add <u>who</u> or <u>that</u> to this conversation where necessary.*
Put an ✗ where <u>who</u> or <u>that</u> is not necessary.

A: I'm looking for someone ____✗____ I can go on vacation with.

B: Hmm. So you want someone _____ is easygoing and independent.

A: Right. But I'd also like a person _____ is reliable.

And I want someone _____ I know well.

B: So why don't you ask me?

A: You? I know you *too* well!

B: Does that mean you think I'm someone _____ is high-strung, dependent, and unreliable?

A: No! I'm just kidding. You're definitely someone _____ I could go on vacation with.

4 *Add <u>who</u> or <u>that</u> where necessary.*

1. My Aunt Jackie is someone I really enjoy spending time with. She's
a person ^who^ loves animals. And although she's someone likes to spend

a lot of time alone, she's very sociable at parties. I admire her

because I like people are independent.

2. Kate is one of the women I work with. She's someone is easygoing

and gets along well with almost everyone. I really like her because

she's someone I can talk to about anything. Unfortunately, Kate

doesn't like her job because her boss is this man is very moody.

I hope Kate can find a new job she likes soon.

5 Heights of fashion

A Do you think your sign influences the way you dress?
Read this Chinese horoscope chart.

Because Chinese New Year falls in January or February, the sign for someone born in either month could be the sign for the preceding year.

The Dog
1946 1958 1970 1982 1994
You like it when people like you. If you are a woman, you are neat and very stylish. If you are a man, you are no different.

The Rooster
1945 1957 1969 1981 1993
Your hair is very important to you. Women who are born in these years always think first about their hair, and they don't care about their wardrobe. If you are a man, you are very similar.

The Monkey
1944 1956 1968 1980 1992
If you are a woman, you have a large wardrobe, and you like to impress people with your choice of clothes. If you are a man, you don't worry too much about what you wear.

The Goat
1943 1955 1967 1979 1991
If you are a woman, you love to dress in style and with taste, and you have a very large closet. If you are a man, you really like to wear designer clothes.

The Pig
1947 1959 1971 1983 1995
Whether you are a man or a woman, you love dressing up. You are sociable, and you like to go to parties to show off your new clothes. If others don't notice them, you get upset.

The Horse
1942 1954 1966 1978 1990
You like elegance, and you follow the latest fashions. If you are a woman, you know this already; however, if you are a man, it may take you a while to realize this.

The Rat
1948 1960 1972 1984 1996
If you are a woman, you don't dress to impress people. But you like it when people notice your charm. If you are a man, you often wear what you threw on the floor the night before.

The Snake
1941 1953 1965 1977 1989
Women like to wear a lot of jewelry and other accessories. If you are a man, you think carefully about what you wear, and you have very good taste.

The Buffalo
1949 1961 1973 1985 1997
You are a practical woman. You like to wear functional clothes during the day and dress much more colorfully at night. If you are a man, you are simply not interested in clothes.

The Tiger
1950 1962 1974 1986 1998
You are the kind of woman who likes to wear strong colors or an unusual piece of jewelry. If you are a man, you like it when you dress differently from other men. When others have suits on, you'll wear jeans and a sweater.

The Cat
1939 1951 1963 1975 1987
Women usually have lovely hair and like beautiful things. They choose clothes carefully. Men are fussy about dressing and follow the latest trends.

The Dragon
1940 1952 1964 1976 1988
You are the kind of person who likes people to notice you, so you sometimes wear unusual clothes. Also, you often have trouble finding comfortable shoes, so you like to go barefoot.

B Find the year of your birth and sign. What does it say about you?
Do you agree? What do you think the signs for these people could be?

1. Steve's friends think he wears strange clothes.
His favorite outfit is a bright yellow jacket with
green slacks and a purple tie. When Steve is at home,
he often doesn't wear shoes.   Sign: _____

2. Wanda loves to wear new clothes when she goes out.
However, she gets really moody if people don't compliment
her on what she's wearing.   Sign: _____

3. Carl is the sort of man who doesn't pay much attention
to his clothes, but his hair always looks great. He goes
to the best salon in town.   Sign: _____

4. Stephanie is someone who always wears extremely bright
colors. She also usually wears an interesting necklace
and earrings.   Sign: _____

6 **Match the clauses in column A with the most suitable clauses in column B.**

A	B
1. I like it _____	**a.** when someone criticizes me in front of other people.
2. I don't mind it _____	**b.** when people are easygoing and friendly.
3. It really upsets me _____	**c.** when rich people are stingy.
4. It embarrasses me _____	**d.** when people are a few minutes late for an appointment.

7 **Write sentences about these situations. Use the expressions in the box.**

I love it . . . .　　　It really bothers me . . . .
It's so irritating . . . .　　It upsets me . . . .
I can't stand it . . . .　　It makes me happy . . . .

1. *It really bothers me when someone pushes in front of me in a line.*

2. _____

3. _____

4. _____

5. _____

6. _____

8 *What are some things you like and don't like about people? Write two sentences about each of the following. Use the ideas in the pictures and your own ideas.*

1. What I really like:

   I love it when someone gives me flowers.

   It makes me happy when _____

   _____

   _____

3. What I don't like:

   It bothers me when _____

   _____

   _____

   _____

2. What really doesn't bother me:

   I really don't mind it when _____

   _____

   _____

4. What upsets or embarrasses me:

   It upsets me when _____

   _____

   _____

9 *It really bugs me!*

Choose one of the things from Exercise 8 that really embarrasses, bothers, or upsets you. Write two short paragraphs about it. In the first paragraph, describe the situation. In the second paragraph, say why this situation is difficult for you and describe a situation you would prefer.

> *It really embarrasses me when someone is very generous to me. Recently, I dated a guy who was always giving me things. For my birthday, he bought me a new CD player, and he treated me to dinner and a movie.*
>
> *The problem is I don't have enough money to treat him in the same way. I'd prefer to date someone I have more in common with. In fact, I'd prefer to date someone who has very little money!*

_____

_____

_____

_____

_____

_____

_____

10 *Choose the correct word to complete each sentence.*

1. I can tell Simon anything, and I know he won't tell anyone else.

   I can really _____ him. (believe/treat/trust)

2. Rita is always _____ people. She can never find anything positive to say about anyone. (arranging/complimenting/criticizing)

3. It bothers me when people are indirect. I prefer people who are

   _____ . (irritating/rude/straightforward)

4. I like it when someone expresses strong _____ . Other people's opinions can really make you think. (accomplishments/conversationalists/views)

5. Jackie is very rich, but she only spends her money on herself.

   She's very _____ . (generous/modest/stingy)

2 Career moves

1

Match the words in column A with the information in column B.

A/An . . .	is a person who . . . .
1. archaeologist _c_	**a.** studies health problems and looks for cures
2. artist _____	**b.** writes articles for newspapers and magazines
3. astronaut _____	✓**c.** studies ancient cultures, people, and places
4. interviewer _____	**d.** asks people questions for stories in newspapers and magazines, or on radio and TV programs
5. journalist _____	
6. medical researcher _____	**e.** leads an orchestra or choir, often in classical music
7. set designer _____	**f.** paints, draws, or makes sculptures
8. conductor _____	**g.** travels into space
	h. creates stage scenery and backgrounds for films

2

Challenging or nerve-racking?

A Complete the chart. Which words have a positive meaning and which ones have a negative meaning?

✓ awful   ☐ boring   ☐ challenging   ☐ dangerous   ☐ difficult
✓ exciting   ☐ fantastic   ☐ interesting   ☐ nerve-racking   ☐ rewarding

Positive	Negative
exciting	_awful_
_____	_____
_____	_____
_____	_____
_____	_____

studying ancient cultures

B Write about three jobs you know. Use the words in part A and gerund phrases.

Example: *I think studying ancient cultures, people, and places could be dangerous!*

1. _____

2. _____

3. _____

3 Career choices

A Match each career and the most appropriate job responsibility.

Careers	Job responsibilities
work for an airline	do research
with computers	keep fit
as a sports instructor	learn new software programs
be a university professor	spend a lot of time alone
a writer	travel to different countries

being a writer

B Use the information from part A and gerund phrases to complete this conversation.

Ann: So, what kind of career would you like, Tom?

Tom: Well, I'm not sure exactly. _Being a writer_ could be interesting. You know, writing novels or perhaps plays.

Ann: The work sounds interesting. But I wouldn't like it because I'd hate _____

_____ and always sitting down.

Tom: What do you want to do, then?

Ann: Well, I'd love _____

_____ . I really like to stay in shape.

Tom: Yeah, I'd like _____ while I worked. You know,

I think I'd also love _____ . Teaching

college students, _____ , and writing

articles would be really rewarding.

Ann: Sure, but don't you think it would be kind of boring?

C Write a short conversation like the one in part B. Use the remaining information in part A or your own ideas.

A: So what kind of career would you like?

B: Well, I'm not exactly sure. _____

A: The work sounds interesting. But I wouldn't like it because _____

B: What do you want to do, then?

A: Well, I'd love _____

B: _____

A: _____

4 *What a job!*

A Read the interviews. Write the correct job title above each interview.

Tell Us About Your Job.

graphic designer

freelance artist

housepainter

musician

orchestra conductor

self-employed builder

1. _____

All my friends seem to earn more than I do. I suppose it's easier if you're employed in a regular 9 to 5 job. I work on people's houses and manage construction sites all day. I stay pretty fit doing that. Then in the evenings and on weekends, I have to make phone calls about jobs and do paperwork. It never seems to end!

2. _____

Working for yourself is hard because you are responsible for everything. If no one calls you and asks you to work for them, you have to go out and look for work. Luckily, I now have some regular clients. I paint pictures for some expensive hotels. Right now, I'm doing some pictures for the rooms of a new hotel in Hawaii.

3. _____

My friends say my work is less demanding than theirs, but I think I work just as hard as they do. I spend a lot of time alone because my job can't begin until all the construction work is completed. Usually, the rooms look great when I've finished my work. Sometimes, though, customers choose really ugly wallpaper and absolutely horrible colors, but I have to do what they want.

4. _____

It would be impossible for me to do my job on my own. The musicians I work with are extremely talented, and they rely on me to make sure they sound as good as possible. We often work evenings and weekends, and we travel a lot. Working with a large number of other people can be challenging, and it really bothers me if someone is moody because it affects everyone else.

B Which of these jobs would you most enjoy doing? Why?

5 First, use words from the list to complete the name of each job title. Then choose the best expressions to compare the jobs in each sentence.

| ☐ assistant | ☐ instructor | ☐ painter | ☑ sitter |
| ☐ guide | ☐ operator | ☐ ranger | ☐ walker |

1. A baby-*sitter* _____ doesn't earn _____ *as much as* _____ a teacher.
   ☑ as much as   ☐ greater than   ☐ worse than

2. A chef's _____ has _____ a waiter.
   ☐ as bad hours as   ☐ not as good hours as   ☐ worse hours than

3. A dog _____ is _____ a student intern.
   ☐ more interesting than ☐ not as boring as   ☐ better paid than

4. A house_____ earns _____ a camp counselor.
   ☐ as bad as   ☐ more than   ☐ not more than

5. A park _____ is _____ a landscaper.
   ☐ as bad as   ☐ not as well paid as   ☐ worse than

6. Being a sports _____ is _____ being a university professor.
   ☐ more than   ☐ as much as   ☐ not as difficult as

7. Being a telephone _____ is _____ being a sales assistant.
   ☐ greater than   ☐ earns more than   ☐ less interesting than

8. A tour _____ has _____ an office worker.
   ☐ longer hours than   ☐ not more than   ☐ not as long as

6 Complete these sentences with the correct prepositions.

| ☐ as | ☐ at | ☐ in | ☐ on | ☐ with |

1. Wai-Man works _____ the best Chinese restaurant in Vancouver.

2. I think working _____ other people is more fun than working alone.

3. I would hate working _____ the media. It would be nerve-racking!

4. Working _____ a dance instructor sounds great.

5. Working in an office is less interesting than working _____ a cruise ship.

7 **Use the words in parentheses to compare the jobs.**

> **Assistant** needed at an outdoor swimming pool. Must be able to swim. Responsible for keeping pool and changing rooms clean. $6/hour. Tues.–Fri. 12–7.

> **Learn computer programming!** In search of a bright young person to work as an intern for a computer company. Some clerical work. $8/hour. Mon.–Fri. 9–5.

1. A: *An assistant at a swimming pool has shorter hours than an intern.*
   (shorter hours)

   B: *Yes, but working as an intern is more interesting than being a swimming pool assistant.*
   (interesting)

> **Travel agency** needs energetic people. Knowledge of a second language is a plus. Mostly answering the phone. $10/hour. Flexible hours. Three vacation days.

> **Tutors** in math, science, English, and music wanted at private summer school. Challenging work with gifted teenagers. Salary negotiable. Mon.–Sat. 3–7.

2. A: *Working in a* _____
   (better benefits)

   B: *Yes, but working* _____
   (challenging)

> **Tennis instructor** needed at summer camp for 12- and 13-year-olds. Must be excellent tennis player and good with kids. $5/hour. Mon.–Fri. 1–7.

> Tour company seeks **guide** to lead bus tours. Great attitude and good speaking voice a must! Fun work, but must be willing to work long hours. $10/hour.

3. A: _____
   (not/much)

   B: _____
   (longer hours)

> Factory seeks **assembly-line** workers to do unskilled work. No experience necessary. $20/hour. Mon.–Thu. 7A.M.–4P.M.

> **Office assistant** required in small, friendly office. Computer skills an advantage. Interesting work. Some management skills necessary. $15/hour. 6-day week.

4. A: _____
   (a shorter work week)

   B: _____
   (less boring)

11

8 *Choose four pairs of jobs to compare. Say which job you would prefer and give two reasons.*

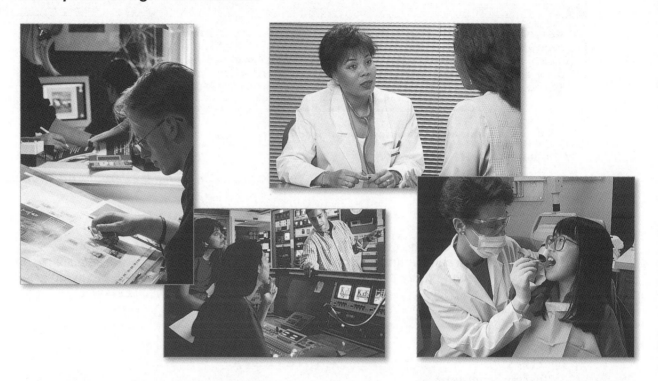

▼ a graphic designer/a TV news director   ▼ a keyboarder/a computer programmer
▼ an archaeologist/a teacher   ▼ a gardener/a landscaper
▼ a doctor/a dentist   ▼ working on a construction site/working in an office
▼ a conductor/a musician   ▼ being self-employed/working for a company

Example: *Working as a TV news director sounds more interesting than being a graphic designer. A TV news director has more responsibility than a graphic designer. Also, directing the news is better paid.*

1. _____

_____

_____

2. _____

_____

_____

3. _____

_____

_____

4. _____

_____

_____

3 Could you do me a favor?

1 Would you mind . . . ?

A Complete the request for each situation.

1. You want to borrow a dollar from a friend for a cup of coffee.
   Can I borrow a dollar for a cup of coffee?

2. You want a classmate to give you a ride home after class.
   Would you mind _____

3. You want to turn down your roommate's radio.
   Is it OK if _____

4. You want to use a friend's phone.
   Do you mind if _____

5. You want to borrow a friend's car for the weekend.
   Would it be OK if _____

6. You want someone to tell you how to get to the subway.
   I was wondering if _____

B Think of four things you would need to have done if you were going on a long vacation. Write requests asking a friend to do the things.

Example: *Could you water the plants?* _____

1. _____
2. _____
3. _____
4. _____

13

2 *Accept or decline these requests. For requests you decline, give excuses. Use the expressions in the box or expressions of your own.*

Accepting	Declining
That's OK, I guess.	Sorry, but . . . .
I'd be glad to.	I'd like to, but . . . .
Fine. No problem.	

1. A: Can I use your computer? I have to type a paper.
   B: *Sorry, but I'm going to use it myself in a few minutes.*

2. A: I've just finished this ten-page paper. Could you check it for me, please?
   B: _____

3. A: I wonder if I could stay overnight at your place.
   B: _____

4. A: Would you mind if I used your phone to make a long-distance call to Nigeria?
   B: _____

3 *Look at the pictures and write the conversations. Speaker A makes a request. Speaker B declines it. Each speaker should give a reason.*

1. A: *I was wondering if you'd mind carrying these suitcases for me. I have a bad back.*
   B: *Sorry, but I have a bad back, too.*

2. A: _____
   B: _____

3. A: _____
   B: _____

4 *Getting what you want*

A Read this magazine article about making requests.

Requests That Get RESULTS

*T*here are many different ways of making requests. For example, if someone wants to borrow a dollar, he or she can say:

"Could you lend me a dollar?"
"Do you have a dollar?"
"You don't have a dollar, do you?"

How does a person know which request to use? Language researchers have suggested that speakers must make several important decisions. First, they must consider the other person's feelings because requests can sometimes cause embarrassment to both the speaker and the listener. If the speaker thinks the listener will accept the request, he or she will probably use a less formal request; however, if the speaker thinks the listener may decline the request, he or she will probably use a fairly formal request. The listener then has to make a choice either to accept or refuse the request. If he or she refuses, then both the speaker and the listener might be embarrassed.

In addition, speakers must decide how well they know the person they are requesting something from and choose a suitable question. If the speaker knows the listener well, one of several types of requests can be used.

For example:
1. Make a statement with *need:* "I need a dollar."
2. Use an imperative: "Please lend me a dollar."
3. Use a question: "Do you have a dollar?"

If the speaker doesn't know the listener well, one of several types of requests can be used instead. For example:
4. Ask about ability: "Could/Can you lend me a dollar?"
5. Use *may:* "May I borrow a dollar?"
6. Ask for permission: "Would it be OK if I borrowed a dollar?"
7. Express curiosity: "I wonder if I could borrow a dollar."
8. State the request negatively: "I don't suppose you could lend me a dollar."
9. Apologize: "I hope you don't mind my asking you for a dollar?"
10. Give a hint: "I wish I had a dollar."

Knowing how to make requests means knowing different types of requests as well as when each type of request is appropriate.

B Check (✓) if each request is less formal or more formal. Then write the correct number from the article (1–10) for each type of request.

	Less formal	More formal	Type
1. Close the door.	☐	☐	_____
2. It's really cold in here.	☐	☐	_____
3. Could you possibly move your car?	☐	☐	_____
4. May I borrow your dictionary?	☐	☐	_____
5. I wonder if you could help me with this assignment.	☐	☐	_____
6. I need some help moving to my new apartment.	☐	☐	_____

C When do you usually use each type of request? Which of the ten types of requests described in the article do you use most often? least often?

5 *Nouns and verbs*

A Complete this chart. Then check your answers in a dictionary.

Noun	Verb	Noun	Verb
accusation	*accuse*	invitation	
apology		permission	
compliment		request	
explanation			

I really like your new haircut.

B Check (✓) the phrase that describes what each person is doing.

1. I really like your new haircut.
   - ☐ giving a reason
   - ✓ giving a compliment

2. You took $20 from my wallet!
   - ☐ making an accusation
   - ☐ offering an apology

3. Sure, you can borrow my computer.
   - ☐ making a request
   - ☐ giving permission

4. I can't lend you my bike because I need it myself.
   - ☐ offering an explanation
   - ☐ accepting an invitation

5. I was wondering if you'd mind helping me cook dinner.
   - ☐ making a request
   - ☐ declining a request

6 *Choose the correct words.*

1. My phone didn't work for a week. The phone company

   _____ an apology and took $50 off my bill.

   (accepted/declined/offered)

2. Peggy told the police that Tony had stolen her car, but Tony totally

   _____ the accusation.   (denied/refused/returned)

3. I forgot to go to Eva's party. When I told her I was sorry, she

   angrily _____ my apology. What more could I do?

   (denied/received/rejected)

4. I told the teacher that I couldn't go to the class party

   because I was sick. She _____ my excuse.

   (accepted/offered/returned)

7 **Use these messages to complete the phone conversations.**
Use indirect requests.

1. A: Is Rosa there, please?
   B: No, she isn't. Would you like to leave a message?
   A: Yes, please. This is Anita calling from Toronto.

   Could you tell _her that my flight arrives at 7 P.M. on Tuesday_ ?

   Would _____ ?
   B: OK, I'll give her the message.

2. A: Can I speak to Eric, please?
   B: I'm afraid he's not here. Do you want to leave a message?
   A: Yes, please. This is Kevin.

   Please _____ .

   And if it's OK, could you _____ ?
   B: Sure, I'll leave him the message.

3. A: Could I speak to Alex, please?
   B: I'm sorry, but he's not here right now.
   A: Oh, OK. This is Judy. I'd like to leave a message.

   Could _____ ?

   Can _____ ?
   B: OK, Judy, I'll give him your message.

4. A: I'd like to speak to Jenny, please.
   B: She's not here right now. Can I take a message?
   A: Yeah. This is Philip.

   Can _____ ?

   And would _____ ?

   Oh, and please _____ .
   B: OK, Philip, I'll give Jenny your message.

8 Complete the conversation with the information in the box. Add any words necessary and use the correct form of the verbs given.

☐ ask Jill to get some soda ☐ bring a big salad
☐ borrow some money ☐ can buy dessert
☑ borrow your CD player ☐ don't be late

Chris: So, is there anything I can do to help?

Len: Yeah. Would it be OK *if I borrowed your CD player* ?
We need good stereo sound at the party.

Chris: Sure. And I'll bring some CDs. I have some great party music.

Len: Thanks.

Chris: No problem. Now, what about food?

Len: Well, I thought maybe a salad. Would you mind

_____ , too?

Chris: Well, OK. And, how about drinks?

Len: Well, I was also wondering if you'd mind

_____ . And please

tell her _____ . Last time we had a party,

she didn't arrive till eleven o'clock, and everyone got really thirsty!

Chris: I remember.

Len: One more thing, I wonder if you

_____ .

Chris: Um. Sure. All right. But, uh, would you mind if I

_____ to pay for it?

9 Rewrite these sentences. Find another way to say each sentence using the words given.

1. Can I use your phone?
   Is it OK if I use your phone? or *Would it be OK if I used your phone?*   (OK)

2. Please ask Penny to stop by and talk to me.

   _____ (would)

3. Could I borrow your guitar?

   _____ (wonder)

4. Would you ask Adam what time he's coming over?

   _____ (could/when)

5. Lend me your hairbrush.

   _____ (mind)

4 What a story!

1 *Complete these news stories using the verbs from the list.*

✓ carrying	☐ missed	☐ disappearing	☐ reported
☐ had	☐ said	☐ happened	

1.

Aircraft in Near Collision

On Tuesday, a jumbo jet that was ___carrying___ 382 passengers and an Air Force plane _____ each other by 15 meters in mid-air over the Atlantic Ocean. A spokesperson for the airline company, which _____ the near miss in a statement yesterday, said the incident _____ so quickly that neither pilot _____ time to take evasive action. "There was no warning whatsoever," _____ the captain of the jumbo jet. He looked out of the window and saw the tail of the Air Force plane as it was _____ into the clouds.

☐ felt	☐ passing	☐ turned	☐ jogging	☐ thought
☐ got	☐ said	☐ gave	☐ realized	

2.

JOGGER GETS SHOCK

A jogger _____ the shock of his life when he was _____ around a city park on Saturday. "As I was _____ under the branches of a large tree, I _____ something drop on me," he recalled. "At first, I _____ it was some branches, but then I _____ it was a snake! I couldn't believe it! Then the guy running ahead of me _____ around and saw it slide off. The snake wasn't particularly big, but it _____ me quite a shock all the same." A snake expert _____ the snake was probably a python, which is non-poisonous.

2 **Match the sentences in columns A and B. Then rewrite the sentences. Join them by using <u>as</u>, <u>when</u>, or <u>while</u>.**

A	B
1. I was crossing the road. _b_	a. My racquet broke.
2. I was using my computer. _____	✓b. A car nearly hit me.
3. We were playing tennis. _____	c. The water went cold.
4. I was taking a shower. _____	d. I burned my finger.
5. I was cooking dinner. _____	e. It suddenly stopped working.

1. _As I was crossing the road, a car nearly hit me._
2. _____
3. _____
4. _____
5. _____

3 **Complete these conversations. Use the past tense or the past continuous of the verbs given.**

1. A: Guess what happened to me last night. As I ___was getting___ (get) into bed, I _____ (hear) a loud noise like a gunshot in the street. Then the phone _____ (ring).

   B: Who was it?

   A: It was Mariana. She always calls me late at night, but this time she had a reason. She _____ (drive) right past my apartment when she _____ (get) a flat tire. It was very late, so while we _____ (change) the tire, I _____ (invite) her to spend the night.

2. A: I'm sorry I'm so late, Kathy. I was at the dentist.

   B: Don't tell me! You _____ (meet) someone interesting while you _____ (sit) in the waiting room. I know how you are, Tom!

   A: Well, you're wrong this time. The dentist _____ (take) X rays when she suddenly _____ (get) called away for an emergency. So I just sat there waiting for two hours!

4 *Lost and found*

A Read this story from a newspaper.

Fishermen found safe and sound

The Taiwanese fishermen were rescued yesterday from a small uninhabited island in the South Pacific. The men had disappeared for more than three months.

They had left Taiwan in a small fishing boat and had planned a week-long trip. On their fifth day, however, they encountered a typhoon, and it badly damaged their boat. Fortunately, none of the men was hurt. After the storm had passed, though, they discovered that the engine wouldn't start, so their boat just drifted at sea for over a month. During this time, the fishermen caught fish to eat and drank rain water to stay alive.

Finally, the boat drifted toward a small island. When it got close enough, the men jumped out and swam to shore. On the island, they found fresh fruit and vegetables, and they continued to catch fish to eat.

The fishermen had lived on the island for two months when a passing ship rescued them. Although the three men had lost a lot of weight, they were still in fairly good shape. Their families feared that the fishermen had lost their lives during the typhoon. They were surprised and happy that the ship had found them and that they were "safe and sound."

B Answer these questions.

1. How long were the fishermen missing?

_____

2. Where did they sail from?

_____

3. How long had they planned to be away?

_____

4. How was the boat damaged in the storm?

_____

5. What did they do to stay alive?

_____

6. How were they rescued?

_____

5 Imagine you got lost like the men in the reading in Exercise 4. Write two
paragraphs about what happened. In the first paragraph, describe
how you got lost. In the second,
say how you got home.

Where were you when you
   got lost? What were you doing?
How long were you lost?
What did you do to find your
   way back?
Were you rescued? How?

> A couple of years ago, I got lost in the mountains. I was
> hiking when it suddenly got foggy. I was really frightened because
> I couldn't see anything, and it was getting cold. I decided to put up
> my tent and stay there for the night.
>   While I was putting up my tent, though, the fog began to clear. . . .

_____

_____

_____

_____

_____

_____

6 Choose the correct verbs to complete the story.

> **Grammar note: After**
>
> In sentences using *after* that show one past event occurring before another,
> the clause with *after* usually uses the past perfect.
> **After** the storm **had passed**, the men discovered that the engine wouldn't start.

Robbie and I ___*had just gotten*___ engaged, so we went to a jewelry store to choose a
              (just got/had just gotten)

wedding ring. I _____ a really nice diamond ring when a man with a mask
                (just chose/had just chosen)

and a gun _____ . After the robber _____ Robbie's wallet,
          (came in/had come in)   (took/had taken)

he _____ the ring. I _____ it to him when the alarm
   (demanded/had demanded)   (just handed/had just handed)

_____ to go off, and the robber _____ . We were so
(started/had started)   (ran off/had run off)

relieved! But then the sales assistant _____ us we had to pay for the ring
                                       (told/had told)

because I _____ it to the robber! We _____ the sales
          (gave/had given)   (just told/had just told)

assistant that we wouldn't pay for it when the police _____ and
                                                      (arrived/had arrived)

_____ us! I've never had such a terrible experience!
(arrested/had arrested)

7 Choose the best headline for each of these events.

What a disaster!

What a predicament!

What an emergency!

What a triumph!

What a lucky break!

1. _____

Joan Smith was seven months pregnant when she and her husband, Hank, went on vacation to a small, remote island. They had had a wonderful first day on the island, but that night Joan was in a lot of pain. There were no doctors on the island, and the hotel where they were staying didn't even have a phone. Hank had almost given up when he finally found the only phone on the island. He called a hospital on the mainland, and half an hour later a helicopter picked Joan up and took her to the hospital – just in time for her to have a beautiful baby girl.

2. _____

Victoria Peters was very sick for several months before her final exams this summer. She simply couldn't study at all. Her parents suggested she should skip a year and take the exams the next summer. Remarkably, Victoria got well suddenly just before the exams, spent the next two weeks studying, and got the highest grade in her class!

3. _____

Jesse Peterson had waited years for a promotion. Finally, a week ago, he was offered the position he had always wanted – Regional Manager. On the same day, however, he won over $16 million in the lottery. Jesse's wife wants him to resign from his job and take her on a trip around the world. Jesse says he cannot decide what to do.

8 Complete the sentences. Use the simple past, the past continuous, or the past perfect of the verbs given.

1. A month after an art show ___*opened*___ (open) in New York, it was discovered that someone _____ (hang) a famous painting by the French painter Henri Matisse upside-down.

2. In 1960, a Turkish diver _____ (discover) the remains of a 3,000-year-old shipwreck while he _____ (dive) for sponges off the coast of southwest Turkey.

3. Several years ago, construction workers _____ (discover) the ruins of Shakespeare's Rose Theatre in London while they _____ (prepare) the site for a new office building.

4. In 1995, an earthquake _____ (strike) Kobe, Japan. An earthquake _____ (not strike) the city for a very long time.

9 *Read this situation. Then use the information and clues to complete the chart. Write the name of each reporter and each country. (You will leave one square in the chart blank.)*

Ms. Anderson

Ms. Benson

Mr. Jackson

Mr. Marks

Mr. Swire

Five news reporters – two women and three men – arrived for an international conference on Sunday, Monday, and Tuesday. No more than two people came on the same day. The reporters came from five different countries.

Clues

The women:	Ms. Anderson and Ms. Benson
The men:	Mr. Jackson, Mr. Marks, and Mr. Swire
The countries:	Australia, Canada, Italy, Singapore, and the United States

The order of arrivals:

- Mr. Swire arrived late at night. No one else had arrived that day.
- Ms. Anderson and Mr. Marks arrived on the same day. The man from Singapore had arrived the day before.
- The reporters from Italy and Australia arrived on the same day.
- Mr. Jackson and the woman from Italy arrived on Tuesday, after Mr. Marks.
- The reporter from Australia had arrived the day after the person from the United States.
- Mr. Marks is from North America but not the United States.

Reporters' Countries and Arrival Days		
Sunday	Name: _____	Name: _____
	Country: _____	Country: _____
Monday	Name: _____	Name: _____
	Country: _____	Country: _____
Tuesday	Name: _____	Name: _____
	Country: _____	Country: _____

5 Crossing cultures

1 Complete these sentences. Use words from the list.

☐ confident ☐ depressed ☑ embarrassed ☐ fascinated ☐ uncomfortable

1. In my country, people never leave tips. So when I first went abroad,
   I kept forgetting to tip waiters. I felt really _embarrassed_ .

2. The first time I traveled abroad, I felt really _____ .
   I was alone, I didn't speak the language, and I didn't make any friends.

3. I just spent a year in France learning to speak French. It was a
   satisfying experience, and I was _____ by the culture.

4. At first I really didn't like shopping in the open-air markets. I felt
   _____ because so many people were trying to sell
   me something at the same time.

5. When I arrived in Lisbon, I was nervous because I couldn't speak any
   Portuguese. As I began to learn the language, though, I became more
   _____ about living there.

2 Respond to the questions about traveling. Write complete sentences using one thing, the (only) thing, or something.

1. Would you be uncomfortable with leaving your family?
   One thing I'd be uncomfortable with is leaving my family.
   or _Leaving my family is something I'd be comfortable with._

2. Would you feel comfortable about traveling alone?
   _____

3. Would you be enthusiastic about making new friends?
   _____

4. Would you be curious about the way people live in other places?
   _____

5. Would you be anxious about spending too much money?
   _____

3 *Imagine you are going to travel to a country you have never visited before. Write sentences using the factors and feelings given. Then add another sentence explaining your feelings.*

Factors	Feelings	
public transportation	anxious (about)	secure (about)
the architecture	comfortable (about)	sure (of)
the food	curious (about)	uncertain (about)
the language	enthusiastic (about)	worried (about)
the money	nervous (about)	

Example: *Public transportation is something I'd be anxious about. I'd be afraid of getting lost.*

1. _____

   _____

2. _____

   _____

3. _____

   _____

4. _____

   _____

4 *Write about living in a foreign country. In the first paragraph, write about the things you would enjoy. In the second paragraph, write about the things you would have difficulty with.*

Mister Twister in Moscow, Russia

    If I lived in a foreign country, learning about the different "music scene" — the bands and singers who are popular — is something I'd enjoy. Another thing I'd be fascinated by is . . . .

    The language, however, is the thing that I'd have the most difficulty with. I find it really hard to learn other languages. The thing about it that would scare me the most is . . . .

_____

_____

_____

_____

_____

5 Culture shock!

A What two main differences have you noticed between your own culture and another one?

B Read this article. Does the article make you think of any other differences?

Each society has its own beliefs, attitudes, customs, behaviors, and social habits. These give people a sense of who they are, how they are supposed to behave, and what they should or should not do.

People become conscious of such rules when they meet people from different cultures. For example, the rules about when to eat vary from culture to culture. Many North Americans and Europeans organize their timetables around three mealtimes a day. In other countries, on the other hand, it's not the custom to have strict rules like this – people eat when they want to, and every family has its own timetable.

When people visit or live in a country for the first time, they are often surprised at the differences that exist between their own culture and the culture in the other country. For some people, traveling abroad is the thing they enjoy most in life; for others, though, cultural

Here are several things to do in order to avoid culture shock.

1. Avoid quick judgments; try to understand people in another culture from their own point of view.
2. Become aware of what is going on around you, and why.
3. Don't think of your cultural habits as "right" and other people's as "wrong."
4. Be willing to try new things and to have new experiences.
5. Try to appreciate and understand other people's values.
6. Think about your own culture and how it influences your attitudes and actions.
7. Avoid having negative stereotypes about foreigners and cultures.
8. Show interest in as well as respect, sincerity, acceptance, and concern for things that are important to other people.

differences make them feel uncomfortable, frightened, or even insecure. This is known as "culture shock."

When you're visiting a foreign country, it is important to understand and appreciate cultural differences. This can help people avoid misunderstandings, develop friendships more easily, and feel more comfortable when traveling or living abroad.

C Use your own words to write definitions for these words.

1. culture _____

2. culture shock _____

3. stereotypes _____

D Choose two pieces of advice in the reading that you think are the most important for avoiding culture shock. Why do you think they are especially important?

Advice	Why it is important

6 Contrasting customs

A Read the information about the different customs and find five pairs of countries with contrasting customs. Write the countries in the chart.

Country	Custom	Country	Custom
In Australia	People don't leave tips in restaurants.	**In New Zealand**	People usually pay for their own meals in restaurants.
In Brazil	People don't go to bed till very late.	**In Spain**	People are late for most appointments.
In Britain	People don't smoke in a friend's home without asking.	**In Sweden**	People arrive on time for most appointments.
In Canada	People go to bed fairly early on weekdays.	**In Turkey**	People smoke almost anywhere they like.
In Egypt	People allow their hosts to treat them to meals in restaurants.	**In the U.S.**	People leave tips of 15%–20% in most restaurants.

Contrasting customs

Australia and the U.S. _____   _____

_____   _____

B Read these four cross-cultural situations. Write sentences describing what the visitors did wrong. Use the expressions in the box.

you're (not) supposed to	it's (not) the custom to
you're (not) expected to	it's (not) acceptable to

1. Brit is from Sweden. When she was on vacation in Spain, some Spanish friends invited her to dinner at 9:00. She arrived at exactly 9:00, but her friends had not even arrived home yet.
   In Spain, you're expected to _____

   _____

2. Marylou is from the United States. On her first day in Australia, she went to a restaurant. She was so happy with the service that she left a tip of 20%. The waiter was horrified.
   In Australia, _____

   _____

3. Peter is from New Zealand. When he went to Egypt, he was invited to
   dinner at a restaurant. He offered to pay for his dinner. His Egyptian
   friend was pretty upset.
   In Egypt, _____

   _____

4. Bulent is from Turkey. When he visited some friends in Britain, he lit
   a cigarette in their living room. He was very surprised when they
   immediately asked him to smoke outside – in the middle of winter.
   In Britain, _____

   _____

7 *Complete these sentences giving information about customs in a country you know.*

1. If you go for a long ride in a friend's car, *it's the custom to offer to pay some of the expenses.*
2. When a friend graduates from school or college, _____

   _____

3. If you borrow something from a friend, _____

   _____

4. If a friend lends you a large sum of money, _____

   _____

5. When a friend invites you to dinner, _____

   _____

8

What advice would you give travelers with these problems and worries?
Use the expressions in the box.

> One thing to remember is . . . .
> Something to keep in mind is . . . .
> One thing visitors often don't realize is . . . .

1. A: I'd really miss my family.

   B: *One thing to remember is that international phone calls*
   are usually cheaper on weekends.
   _____

2. A: I often get a stomachache when I go abroad.

   B: _____
   _____
   _____

3. A: I'd feel nervous about carrying lots of cash around with me.

   B: _____
   _____
   _____

4. A: I think I'd get suspicious about the prices of some things.

   B: _____
   _____
   _____

5. A: I wouldn't be very sure of myself.

   B: _____
   _____
   _____

6 What's wrong with it?

1 *What can be wrong with these things? Put these words in the correct categories. (Most words go in more than one category.)*

| car | carpet | collar | furniture | glass | pipe | pitcher | tablecloth |

chipped	cracked	dented	leaking	scratched	stained	torn

2 *Something is wrong with each of these things. Write a sentence about each one.*

1. *The car is scratched.*   or
There's a scratch on the car.

2. _____

3. _____

4. _____

5. _____

6. _____

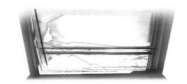 

7. _____

8. _____

9. _____

31

3 Problems, problems, problems!

A Have you ever bought something that didn't work right? What did you do about it? Have you ever had a problem getting a refund? What happened?

B Read about these problems described in *Consumer* magazine.

Consumer
m a g a z i n e

Sharon's computers

Sharon Kurtz is a freelance secretary who works at home. She bought a computer from *Star Superstore*. When she took it home, however, she found that the screen was not clear. The store agreed to exchange it. When a new computer was delivered to her home, Sharon found that the plastic cover was scratched. She complained, and the store offered her a third computer, but this one didn't work right, either. Some of the keys on the keyboard were loose. She was offered a fourth computer, but it stopped working a week after she started using it.

At this point, Sharon got really angry and contacted *Consumer* magazine. We wrote *Star Superstore* a letter explaining that Sharon was losing work because of all the computer problems. The store offered Sharon a full refund plus $1,000 for all the inconvenience she had suffered.

Chris's car

Chris Hill thought his troubles were over when the police found his stolen car, but in fact his problems were only just beginning. The engine was badly damaged, and it needed to be replaced at a cost of $2,300. In addition, the locks were broken, and they needed to be repaired at a cost of $400. Chris's insurance company told him that he would have to pay 40% of the cost of the new engine ($920). They argued that the new engine would add 40% to the value of his car. However, Chris did not believe this.

Chris knew that the value of a used car depends mainly on its age, so he contacted *Consumer* magazine. One of our lawyers asked the insurance company to prove that the new engine would increase the value of the car. When the insurance company replied, they said they no longer wanted Chris to pay any of the repair costs.

C Complete the chart.

	Problems	What *Consumer* magazine did	Compensated? Yes	No
1. Sharon's computers	*unclear screen*		☐	☐
2. Chris's car			☐	☐

4 *Choose suitable verbs to complete the sentences.*
Use passive infinitives or gerunds.

> ### Language note: Verbs ending in -en or -n
>
> Some verbs are formed by adding *-en* or *-n* to a noun or adjective.
> These verbs mean "to make more of something."
>
> | Noun | Verb | | Adjective | Verb |
> |------|------|--|-----------|------|
> | length | → length**en** | | loose | → loose**n** |
> | (make something longer) | | | (make something looser) | |

1

2

3

4

5

6

☑ lengthen   ☐ sharpen   ☐ straighten   ☐ widen   ☐ loosen   ☐ tighten

1. This jacket is too short. It needs <u>*to be lengthened*</u> .

   or It needs <u>*lengthening*</u> .

2. The screws on these glasses are too loose.

   They need _____ .

3. The blades on these scissors are too dull.

   They need _____ .

4. This faucet is too tight.

   It needs _____ .

5. This road has too many dangerous turns.

   It needs _____ .

6. This street is too narrow.

   It needs _____ .

5 Complete the conversation. Use <u>need</u> or <u>needs</u> with passive infinitives (<u>to be</u> + past participle) or gerunds of the verbs given.

Tim: Guess what? Someone broke into my car last night!

Jan: Oh, no. What did they take?

Tim: Nothing! But they did a lot of damage. The lock _needs to be repaired_ . (repair)

And the windows _____ . (replace)

Jan: What about your car radio?

Tim: They broke off the switch. I found the broken piece on the floor.

It just _____ . (glue)

Jan: It was probably some young kids having "fun."

Tim: Yeah, some fun. The seats

_____ . (clean)

I think they had a party in my car!

Jan: How annoying. Does the car drive OK?

Tim: No, it feels strange. The gears aren't shifting right, so

they _____ . (fix) And the

brakes _____ (check) right away.

Jan: Well, I guess you're lucky they didn't steal it!

Tim: Yeah, lucky me.

6 Write about something you have bought that had something wrong with it. In the first paragraph, describe the problem. In the second paragraph, explain what you did about it.

> Recently, I bought a coffee maker. While I was unpacking it, I could see it was damaged. The glass carafe was chipped and needed to be replaced. And to make matters worse, the machine leaked!
>
> I took it back to the store. I was nervous because I had lost my receipt. Luckily, the clerk didn't ask me for it. She said a lot of customers had recently had similar problems, and she gave me a full refund.

7 **Complete this crossword puzzle.**

Across

1 Do you have another _____ for these flowers? This one is cracked.

4 You can't wear this _____ to your job interview, Dave. Two buttons have come off the front, and the lining is torn.

9 This is a great new food _____ . It really helps me chop vegetables more quickly.

11 The buttons on this shirt are _____ . They'll come off if they aren't fixed soon.

12 I spilled coffee on this dress. Now it's badly _____ .

13 These socks have a hole in them. I'd like to _____ them for another pair, please.

14 The glass in that window is _____ . It needs replacing.

Down

2 This carpet is really dirty. It needs to be _____ .

3 The _____ beside your desk needs to be emptied. It's full of paper.

5 There's a _____ in your jeans. Look, the left leg is badly torn.

6 I prefer to cook on a gas _____ than to cook on an electric one.

7 The back of my car is slightly _____ . Someone drove into the back of it.

8 Look! There's a stain on the _____ of the jacket you're wearing – just below your right ear.

10 The paint on my car door is _____ , and it needs repainting. It looks like someone damaged it with a sharp knife.

8 *Jack'll fix it!*

A Match each problem with the repair needed.

Jack's ⊶ Repair Shop

Item	Problem		Repair needed
1. dishwasher	doesn't work ___f___		a. tighten and glue the legs
2. VCR	tape is stuck _____		b. clean and polish the wood
3. speakers	wood covers are damaged _____		c. remove the tape
4. TV	screen is cracked _____		d. repaint the door
5. stove	metal door is scratched _____		e. replace the screen
6. table	table legs are loose _____	✓	f. check the motor

B Write a sentence describing each problem. Then add a sentence describing the repair needed to fix it. Use passive infinitives or gerunds.

1. *The dishwasher doesn't work. The motor needs to be checked.*

   or *The motor needs checking.*

2. _____

   _____

3. _____

   _____

4. _____

   _____

5. _____

   _____

6. _____

   _____

C Think of three items you own that are damaged (or were damaged) in some way. Write a sentence describing each problem. Then write another sentence describing the action needed to fix it.

1. _____

   _____

2. _____

   _____

3. _____

   _____

7 The world we live in

1 *Change these sentences from the active to the passive. Use the expressions given.*

Here are just some of the dangers facing you and your children.

The water we drink
1. Rivers full of dead fish are supplying our drinking water.
2. Additives, such as chlorine, have ruined the taste of our drinking water.

The food we eat
3. Traffic pollution is contaminating agricultural crops such as fruits and vegetables.
4. Agricultural sprays have caused mysterious new illnesses.

The air we breathe
5. Factories are burning extremely dangerous chemicals.
6. Smog has endangered people's lives in many large cities.

The world we live in
7. Global warming has damaged plants and wildlife.
8. Reduced rainfall is creating bigger and bigger deserts.

Join *Save Our Planet* Today

1. *Our drinking water is being supplied by rivers full of dead fish.*   (by)

2. _____
   _____ (due to)

3. _____
   _____ (because of)

4. _____
   _____ (by)

5. _____
   _____ (by)

6. _____
   _____ (as a result of)

7. _____
   _____ (through)

8. _____
   _____ (because of)

2 Verbs and nouns

A Complete the chart.

Verb	Noun	Verb	Noun
contaminate	contamination	educate	_____
contribute	_____	_____	pollution
_____	creation	protect	_____
deplete	_____	_____	reduction
_____	destruction	threaten	_____

B Write four sentences like the ones in Exercise 1 using words from the chart.

Example: _Many rivers and streams have been badly contaminated by industrial waste._

1. _____
2. _____
3. _____
4. _____

3 Choose the correct words or phrases.

El Yunque rain forest

1. Green organizations are trying to save rain forests that have been _____threatened_____ by developers and farmers.   (created/ruined/threatened)

2. One way to inform the public about factories that pollute the environment is through _____ programs on TV.   (agricultural/educational/industrial)

3. The ozone layer has been _____ more in the southern hemisphere than in the northern hemisphere.   (depleted/destroyed/polluted)

4. Agricultural sprays are _____ the soil in many countries.   (damaging/eating up/lowering)

5. _____ is an enormous problem in many large cities where whole families can only afford to live in one room.   (pollution/poverty/waste)

38

4 *How safe are your plastic cards?*

A How many of these cards do you have: a credit card? a store card? an ID card? a debit card? a phone card? a membership card? How many of your cards are made of plastic?

B Read about plastic cards.

It's in the Cards

In recent years, more and more people have been paying for things with credit cards. There are now 565 million credit cards worldwide, but it doesn't stop there. Debit cards are being issued by banks, and store cards are being offered by many department stores. Bills and coins are gradually being replaced by "plastic money." In many countries, phone cards have been introduced for people to use in pay phones. In addition, cards made of paper are being replaced by plastic ones by many organizations and clubs. For example, if you belong to a sports club, your membership card may well be made of plastic.

How safe is the plastic used to make these cards, though? Until now, most cards have been made from a plastic called PVC. While PVC is being produced, harmful chemicals are released into the atmosphere. One of the most dangerous chemicals that is released is dioxin, which is known to cause cancer in humans. A further problem is that, when a PVC card is thrown away, it is not biodegradable; this means that it does not "break down" and cannot be recycled. Obviously, recycling reduces pollution of the environment.

The executive director of the environmental organization and charity *Greenpeace*, Peter Melchett, says, "If there is a solution to this – and an alternative – then it would be madness not to use it." *Greenpeace* has found a solution and an alternative. Their new credit card is made entirely from a biodegradable plastic that uses plants. The card breaks down in around three months in special soil called compost; in this way, it is recycled. In contrast, a PVC card lasts for centuries. *Greenpeace* hopes that many organizations will soon follow their example and issue cards that do not threaten the public health.

C Check (✔) True or False. For statements that are false, write the true information.

	True	False
1. Fewer and fewer credit cards are made of paper.	☐	☐
2. The plastic used in credit cards is fairly safe.	☐	☐
3. Most credit cards are biodegradable.	☐	☐
4. The new credit card that is being introduced by *Greenpeace* is not made of plastic.	☐	☐
5. The new *Greenpeace* card breaks down in a few months.	☐	☐

5 *Choose the correct word or phrase.*

☐ drug trafficking	☐ global warming	☐ poverty
☐ famine	☐ incurable diseases	

1. In my opinion, _____ is the biggest problem today. If we could stop people from selling drugs, no one would be able to buy them.

2. More money should be given to do medical research into _____ , such as Alzheimer's.

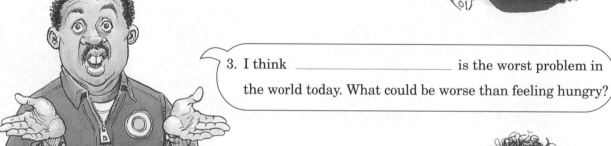

3. I think _____ is the worst problem in the world today. What could be worse than feeling hungry?

4. If we don't stop _____ , temperatures will rise, and many places will become deserts.

5. The best way to improve people's lives is to try to relieve _____ . Everyone should have enough money to buy the things they need.

6 *Complete the conversations. Use the expressions in the box and the information on the list.*

One thing to do	The best thing to do . . . .
Another thing to do	One way to help . . . .

☐ complain to the Parks Department about it
☑ create more government-funded jobs
☐ create more public housing projects
☐ educate young people about its dangers
☐ organize a public meeting to protest the threat to public property
☐ report it to the local newspaper

1. A: There are so many unemployed people in this city. I just don't know what can be done about it.

   B: *One thing to do is to create more government-funded jobs.*

2. A: Personally, I'm worried about drug trafficking. It puts lots of children and young people at risk.

   B: _____

   _____

3. A: You know, there's a lot of corruption in our city government.

   B: _____

   _____

   A: Yeah, the bad publicity might help to clean things up a bit.

4. A: What worries me most is the number of homeless people on the streets.

   B: _____

   _____

5. A: Did you know that a big housing developer wants to build apartments in Forest Hill Park? I think it's terrible.

   B: _____

   _____

   A: That's a good idea.

   B: _____

   _____

drug trafficking

a new housing development?

7 ***Complete the sentences using the passive of the present continuous
or the present perfect. Then suggest solutions to each problem.***

1. Prices <u>*have been raised*</u> (raise) a lot in recent years.

   One way to deal with inflation <u>*is to stop pay raises*</u> .

2. These days, a lot of endangered animals _____ (kill)

   by hunters and poachers. The best way to stop them _____

   _____ .

3. During the past few years, lots of trees _____ (destroy)

   by acid rain. One thing to do about it is _____

   _____ .

4. Underground water _____ (contaminate)

   by agricultural sprays. The best way to deal with the problem _____

   _____ .

8 ***Write two paragraphs about a charity you know about. In the first paragraph,
describe what the charity does. In the second paragraph, explain why you
think the charity is doing useful work.***

Note: Charities are
organizations that
try to solve or reduce
problems in the
world. For example,
some charities work
to help people or
animals in need,
while others deal
with environmental
issues.

>   *A well-known charity in my country is Shelter. The main purpose
> of the organization is to reduce the number of homeless people.
> The charity believes the best way to do this is to provide free or
> inexpensive housing. . . .*
>   *Shelter is my favorite charity because homelessness is, in my
> opinion, the greatest problem facing my country. Many young people
> cannot find jobs, and so they cannot afford to find housing. . . .*

8 Learning to learn

1 Choose the correct words or phrases.

1. I need the _____ to find out if I want to take a music appreciation class.   (course catalog/literature/video equipment)

2. I've always wanted to make things with wood, so I'm going to take a _____ class this semester. (art/carpentry/science)

3. The community college told me it's too late to _____ classes this semester. I'll have to wait and sign up next semester. (attempt/register for/study)

4. I'd love to sing in a _____ , but I'd have to hire a teacher first because my voice is terrible. (choir/orchestra/tutor)

2 Preferences, anyone?

A Write questions with *would rather* or *would prefer* using the cues.

1. take a science class/an art class

   Would you rather take a science class or an art class?

   or _Would you prefer to take a science class or an art class?_

   or _Would you prefer taking a science class to an art class?_

2. study part-time/full-time

   _____

3. have a boring job that pays well/an exciting job that pays less

   _____

4. take a long vacation once a year/several short vacations each year

   _____

B Write answers to the questions you wrote in part A.

1. _____
2. _____
3. _____
4. _____

3 *Love it or leave it*

A First, complete speaker A's questions with four things you
would *not* like to do. Use ideas in the box or your own ideas.

> learn basket weaving
> learn to play the accordion
> learn how to repair appliances
> start your own business
> take a class in geology
> take a poetry appreciation class

Example:

A: Do you want to *learn basket weaving* ?

B: *I'd rather not. I'd prefer to take a class in filmmaking.*

or *I'd prefer not to. I'd rather take a class in filmmaking.*

1. A: Do you want to _____ ?

   B: _____

2. A: Would you like to _____ ?

   B: _____

3. A: Do you want to _____ ?

   B: _____

4. A: Would you like to _____ ?

   B: _____

B Now write responses for speaker B.
For each question, think of something
you would prefer to do. Use the short
answers *I'd rather not* or *I'd prefer not
to* and say what you would prefer to do.

BEGINNER ACCORDION

4 *Answer these questions and give reasons.*

1. On your day off, would you rather stay home or go out?

   I'd rather stay home than go out because _____

2. Would you prefer to have a cat or a dog?

   _____

3. Would you prefer living in an apartment building or in a house?

   _____

4. When you entertain friends, would you rather invite them over
   for dinner or take them out to a restaurant?

5 *Home schooling*

A In some countries, there are children who are educated by their parents at home instead of by teachers at school. Do you think this is a good idea or a bad idea? Think of two advantages and two disadvantages.

B Read the passage and underline the information that answers these questions.

1. How many children in the United States learn at home?
2. Why do some parents prefer to teach their own children?
3. How do the Gutersons choose what to teach their children?
4. What are two criticisms of home schooling?

Home Schooling

All children in the United States have to receive an education, but the law does not say they have to be educated at school. A number of parents prefer not to send their children to school. Children who are educated at home are known as "home-schoolers." There are about 300,000 home-schoolers in the United States today. Some parents prefer teaching their children at home because they do not believe that public schools teach the correct religious values; others believe they can provide a better educational experience for their children by teaching them at home. Interestingly, results show that home-schooled children quite often do better than average on national tests in reading and math.

David Guterson and his wife teach their three children at home. Guterson says that his children learn very differently from children in school. Learning starts with the children's interests and questions. For example, when there is heavy snowfall on a winter day, it may start a discussion or reading about climate, snow removal equipment, Alaska, polar bears, and winter tourism. Or a spring evening when the family is out watching the stars is a good time to ask questions about satellites and the space program. If the Brazilian rain forests are on the TV news, it could be a perfect time to talk about how rain forests influence the climate, how deserts are formed, and how the polar ice caps affect ocean levels.

Home schooling is often more interesting than regular schools, but critics say that home-schoolers are outsiders who might be uncomfortable mixing with other people in adult life. Critics also say that most parents are not well qualified to teach their children. However, most parents don't have the time or the desire to teach their children at home, so schools will continue to be where most children get their formal education.

C What do you think the Gutersons might teach their children if the TV news showed:

1. people without enough food to eat _____

_____

2. a sailor arriving home after sailing alone around the world _____

_____

3. doctors announcing a cure for the common cold _____

_____

6 *Complete the sentences with <u>by (not)</u> + gerund.*
Use the ideas in the box or your own information.

cook at home	join a sports club	exercise regularly	✓ not stay home
eat good food	not eat out	go out more often	use e-mail

cook at home

join a sports club

use e-mail

1. A good way to enjoy the weekend is *by not staying home.*
2. A good way to keep in touch with old friends is
3. You can make new friends
4. The best way to save money is
5. You could stay in shape
6. I stay healthy

7 *Choose the correct words or phrases.*

1. Diana shows her _____ (competitiveness/communications skills/concern for others) by volunteering to help people with incurable diseases.

2. My parents' love of art, poetry, and music taught me _____ . (artistic appreciation/cooperation/perseverance)

3. I learned _____ (concern for others/courtesy/self-confidence) from my parents. They taught me the importance of being polite to both family and friends.

4. Barbara always gets upset with people who disagree with her. I wish she would show more _____ . (perseverance/self-confidence/tolerance)

8 *Choose suitable qualities from the list for the students in these descriptions.*

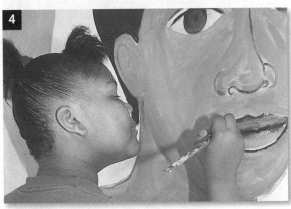

☐ competitiveness   ☐ creativity   ☐ self-confidence
☐ cooperation   ☐ perseverance   ☐ tolerance

1. John is very good at most school subjects, but he has no interest in being "the best." Instead, he is very kind and helpful. The world would be a better place if everyone showed as much _____ as John.

2. Felix finds school very hard, but no one tries harder than he does. He always spends the whole weekend in the library trying to keep up with his studies. He shows great _____ .

3. Betsy always wants to do better than everyone else. In her schoolwork, she always tries to get the best grades. Her favorite sport is badminton because she's the best player in the school. No one needs to teach Betsy _____ .

4. Andrea has more _____ than any of her classmates. She writes fascinating stories that show she has a wonderful imagination. She's also very artistic and does very interesting paintings.

9   *My way*

A List two methods of learning each of these skills.

Skill	Methods
1. become a good guitarist	*by teaching myself* *by taking lessons*
2. learn a new craft	
3. become a good photographer	
4. learn how to drive	
5. become skilled at auto-repair	

my first guitar

ten years later

B Which of the two methods in
part A would you prefer to use to develop each skill?
Write sentences using *would rather (not)* or *would prefer (not)*. Give reasons.

1. *I'd rather learn guitar by teaching myself than by taking lessons.*
   I'd prefer not to take lessons because they're expensive.

2. _____

   _____

3. _____

   _____

4. _____

   _____

5. _____

   _____

9 Self-improvement

1 *Whose services do these people need? Choose the correct words or phrases.*

- ☐ astrologer
- ☐ car detailer
- ☑ fortune-teller
- ☐ genealogist
- ☐ headhunter
- ☐ hypnotherapist
- ☐ interior designer
- ☐ party planner
- ☐ personal shopper

personal shopper

car detailer

interior designer

1. *fortune-teller*

   I'd be interested in having someone predict my future, though I'm not sure that I really believe in all that stuff.

2. _____

   You know how Tina always used to bite her fingernails, just like me? Well, she saw someone who used hypnosis to treat her, and she hasn't bitten her nails since.

3. _____

   I'd really like to know more about my family. I don't even know who my great-grandparents were!

4. _____

   I'd like to have someone read my horoscope.

5. _____

   I haven't been able to find a job for about nine months. I think I'd better find someone to help me.

6. _____

   I want to have all my friends over for a party, but I just don't know how to put it together.

7. _____

   I don't know what to get for my parents' wedding anniversary, and I hate shopping!

8. _____

   Look at my car! It's filthy. I just never have time to clean it myself.

9. _____

   My apartment looks awful. I want to buy new furnishings, but I don't know what will look good. I need help!

2 Collocations

A Match the verbs in column A with the nouns in column B. Write the collocations.

A	B	
☑ check	☐ my computer	1. _check my fitness level_
☐ decorate	☐ my dog	2. _____
☐ fix	☐ my family history	3. _____
☐ tell	☑ my fitness level	4. _____
☐ trace	☐ my fortune	5. _____
☐ train	☐ my home	6. _____

B First, use the items in part A to write questions for speaker A. Use the phrases *Do you know where I can* **have** *someone . . . ?* or *Do you know where I can* **get** *someone* **to** *. . . ?* Then write responses for speaker B using your own ideas.

1. A: _Do you know where I can have someone check my fitness level?_

   B: _Sure. You can have it checked at the free clinic._

or A: _Do you know where I can get someone to check my fitness level?_

   B: _Sure. You can get it checked at the free clinic._

2. A: _____

   B: _____

3. A: _____

   B: _____

4. A: _____

   B: _____

5. A: _____

   B: _____

6. A: _____

   B: _____

3 **Describe where you can have these services done.**
Use the passive with <u>have</u> or <u>get</u>.

COME TO
SALON
2000

FOR THE
BEST HAIRCUT
OF THE
CENTURY.

1. <u>You can have your hair cut at Salon 2000.</u>
   or <u>You can get your hair cut at Salon 2000.</u>

AT
Kwik
Fix
WE REPAIR
ALL KINDS
OF SHOES.

2. _____

DREAM CLEAN

"WE DRY-CLEAN YOUR CLOTHES
LIKE NOBODY ELSE."

3. _____

Crazy Catherine
CAN TELL YOUR FUTURE.

JUST SHOW HER YOUR PALM
AND SHE'LL READ IT.

4. _____

ARE YOUR CARPETS FILTHY?
CALL US AT
Carpet World

AND WE'LL SHAMPOO YOUR
CARPETS SO THEY'RE AS GOOD AS NEW.

5. _____

Feng Shui goes west

A Look at the picture. What do you think a person who practices Feng Shui does?

Feng Shui

For thousands of years, the ancient art form of Feng Shui has played a major role in Chinese life. Feng Shui means "wind and water," and it is based on an appreciation of the relationship between people and the environment. It involves changing the design of your living or working space to improve your fortune.

For instance, soon after a Hong Kong millionaire moved his business to a new skyscraper, his business began to do very badly. He immediately called in Feng Shui experts. They told him that because his new office block was round, it was like a huge cigarette, and all the energy was burning off through the roof. They said that the only thing he could do to prevent this loss of energy was to build a swimming pool on the roof. The millionaire followed their advice, and his business immediately started to do well.

In recent years, Feng Shui has become popular in many western countries, where companies such as B & Q have started to seek advice from Feng Shui experts. Brian Ingliss, the manager of one of B & Q's new hardware stores in Britain, says, "I first encountered Feng Shui when I went to the opening of our company's store in Taiwan. Everyone takes it so seriously, you cannot fail to be impressed." Before his store was opened, he consulted a Feng Shui expert. The expert told him where to put various departments and advised him to create a lot of free space around the store. Brian followed the advice, and, within a year, the store was the most successful B & Q store in the country. Brian concludes, "Some people may think it is just mumbo jumbo, . . . but much of Feng Shui is just common sense."

B Read about Feng Shui. Check (✓) True or False. For statements that are false, write the true information.

	True	False
1. Feng Shui concerns the relationship between humans and the world around them.	☐	☐
2. According to Feng Shui, a round building is good for business.	☐	☐
3. Feng Shui has been popular in western countries for several centuries.	☐	☐
4. Brian Ingliss introduced Feng Shui to B & Q's store in Taiwan.	☐	☐
5. The B & Q store Ingliss manages is the most successful in Britain.	☐	☐

C Write answers to the questions.

1. What do you think of Feng Shui? Is it common sense or "mumbo jumbo"?

2. In what circumstances would you consult a Feng Shui expert?

5   *Make at least one suggestion for each of these problems.*

1. I never have any energy, so I can never do anything except work. I sleep all weekend, so don't tell me to get more rest!

   Have you thought about *taking an aerobics class?*
   Some people say exercise gives them more energy.
   Another thing you could do is improve your diet.

2. My problem is a constant backache. I just don't know what to do to get rid of it. I had someone give me a massage, but it didn't really help.

   Maybe you could _____

   _____

3. My doctor told me to get more exercise. She strongly recommended swimming, but I find swimming so boring! In fact, aren't all sports boring?

   Why don't you _____

   _____

4. I'm very sociable, and I have great difficulty saying "No!" I end up doing things every night of the week – going to parties, discos, the movies. I'm so tired!

   It might be a good idea _____

   _____

5. I like to be a good neighbor, but the woman next door drives me crazy. She's always knocking on my door to talk for hours. And whenever I go out into the yard, she goes into her yard – and talks for hours!

   What about _____

   _____

6

Write questions for speaker A using the passive with have or get. Then write responses for speaker B using the expressions in the box.

What about . . . ?	Why don't you . . . ?
Have you thought about . . . ?	Maybe you could . . . .

1. organize a wedding reception

   A: *Do you know where I can have a wedding organized?*

   B: *What about calling Weddings Unlimited?*

2. repair a bicycle

   A: _____

   B: _____

3. lengthen pants

   A: _____

   B: _____

4. fix a camera

   A: _____

   B: _____

5. replace a watch battery

   A: _____

   B: _____

6. enlarge a gold ring

   A: _____

   B: _____

10 The past and the future

1 Choose the correct words to complete the sentences.

1. No one knows why many ships and planes have disappeared in the Bermuda Triangle in recent years. It's still _____*a mystery*_____ . (a discovery/an expedition/a mystery)

2. Captain James Cook led three _____ to the Pacific and Antarctica from 1768 to 1779.   (assassinations/expeditions/revolutions)

3. The work of many scientists over a period of about 150 years contributed to the _____ of the computer.   (achievement/invention/transformation)

4. Three scientific advances took place during the mid-1890s: the _____ of X rays, radioactivity, and the electron.   (discoveries/explorations/inventions)

5. Landing people on the moon in 1969 was a great _____ in space technology.   (achievement/catastrophe/segregation)

6. In 1995, a powerful earthquake struck Kobe, Japan. It was _____ for people living in the area.   (a catastrophe/an exploration/a population)

2 Complete the sentences. Use words from the list.

ago	during	for	from	in	since	to

jazz

the Berlin Wall

1. Mexico has been independent ___*for*___ nearly 200 years.

2. The telephone was invented over a hundred years _____ .

3. Brasília has been the capital city of Brazil _____ 1960.

4. Electric streetcars were introduced _____ the 1900s.

5. Jazz first became popular _____ the 1920s.

6. World War II lasted _____ 1939 _____ 1945.

7. Vietnam was separated into two parts _____ about 30 years.

8. East and West Germany have been united _____ the Berlin Wall came down.

3 Nouns and verbs

A Complete this chart. Then check your answers in a dictionary.

Noun	Verb	Noun	Verb
assassination	_assassinate_	explosion	_____
demonstration	_____	invention	_____
discovery	_____	revolution	_____
discrimination	_____	segregation	_____
existence	_____	transformation	_____
exploration	_____	vaccine	_____

B Choose verbs from the chart in part A to complete these sentences. Use the correct verb tense.

1. In 1885, Louis Pasteur _____ _discovered_ _____ a cure for rabies when he treated a young boy who was bitten by a dog.

2. Aung San, the man who led Myanmar to independence, was _____ in 1947. No one is certain who killed him.

3. Until the 1960s, there were many laws that _____ against African Americans in many southern states of the United States.

4. The European Union has _____ since 1957. There are now fifteen member states.

5. In the past few years, the computer has _____ our lives in so many different ways. For example, many people now pay their bills through their computers.

6. One of the few parts of the world that has not been _____ much is Antarctica. The extreme climate makes it dangerous to travel far from research centers.

7. In 1986, millions of Filipinos _____ against the government of Ferdinand Marcos in the streets of Manila.

8. In World War I, many soldiers were _____ against the disease typhoid.

Louis Pasteur (1822–1895)

a research station in Antarctica

4 *Vaccines past, present, and future*

A Have you ever had a vaccination? Do you know what diseases you have been vaccinated against?

VACCINATIONS

For well over a thousand years, smallpox was a disease that everyone feared. The disease killed much of the native population in South America when the Spanish arrived there in the early sixteenth century. By the end of the eighteenth century, smallpox was responsible for the deaths of about one in ten people around the world. Those who survived the disease were left with ugly scars on their skin.

It had long been well known among farmers that people who worked with cows rarely caught smallpox; instead, they often caught a similar but much milder disease called cowpox. A British doctor called Edward Jenner was fascinated by this, and so he studied cowpox. He became convinced that, by vaccinating people with the disease, he could protect them against the much worse disease smallpox. In 1796, he vaccinated a boy with cowpox and, two months later, with smallpox. The boy did not get smallpox. In the next two years, Jenner vaccinated several children in the same way, and none of them got the disease.

News of the success of Jenner's work soon spread. In 1800, the Royal Vaccine Institution was founded in Berlin, Germany. In the following year, Napoleon opened a similar institute in Paris, France. Vaccination soon became a common method to protect people against other viral diseases, such as rabies, and vaccines were sent across the world to the United States and India.

It took nearly two centuries to achieve Jenner's dream of getting rid of smallpox from the whole world. In 1967, the World Health Organization (WHO) started an ambitious vaccination program, and the last case of smallpox was recorded in Somalia in 1977. The story of vaccinations does not end there, however. There are many other diseases that kill more and more people every year. In addition, many new diseases are being discovered. The challenge for medical researchers will, therefore, probably continue for several more centuries.

B Read about vaccinations. Complete the chart with the history of events in the story of vaccinations.

Date	Event
1. Early 16th century	*Smallpox killed much of the native population in South America.*
2. End of the 18th century	
3. 1796	
4. 1800	
5. 1967	
6. 1977	

5 *Life in 2030*

A Complete these predictions about life in 2030. Use the future continuous of the verb given. Then add two more predictions of your own.

live on the moon?

By 2030, . . .

1. people _____*will be wearing*_____ temperature-controlled body suits.   (wear)

2. some people _____ in cities on the moon.   (live)

3. people _____ cars that run on electricity.   (drive)

4. people _____ in new types of athletic events in the Olympics.   (compete)

5. _____
   _____

6. _____
   _____

B Complete these predictions about what will have happened by 2030. Use the future perfect. Then add two more predictions of your own.

By 2030, . . .

1. computers _____*will have replaced*_____ people as translators.   (replace)

2. ties for men _____ out of fashion.   (go)

3. scientists _____ a cheap way of getting drinking water from seawater.   (discover)

4. medical researchers _____ a cure for the common cold.   (find)

5. _____
   _____

6. _____
   _____

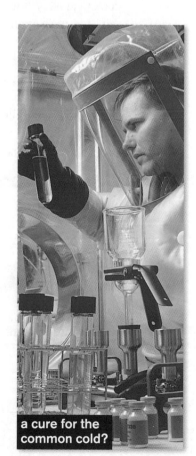

a cure for the common cold?

6 *Write two responses to each question.*

1. What are you doing this weekend?   (Use the present continuous.)
   <u>I'm going out for dinner on Friday evening.</u>
   _____

   _____

2. How will cities of the future be different?   (Use *will* or *won't*.)
   <u>Cities won't allow cars downtown.</u>
   _____

   _____

3. How is your hometown going to change in the next few years?   (Use *be going to*.)
   <u>They're going to build a new airport.</u>
   _____

   _____

4. What will or won't you be doing in ten years?   (Use the future continuous.)
   <u>I won't be living with my parents.</u>
   _____

   _____

5. What advances will scientists have made by 2050?   (Use the future perfect.)
   <u>Scientists will have found a way to grow enough food for everyone.</u>
   _____

   _____

7 *Think of four ways that computers will affect how we live and work in the next 20 years.*

Example: <u>Children will be doing</u>
<u>all their schoolwork on</u>
<u>computers.</u>

1. _____

2. _____

3. _____

4. _____

8 *Write two paragraphs about one of these topics or a topic of your choice. In the first paragraph, briefly describe the past. In the second paragraph, describe how you think the future will be.*

the European Union

Topics	
changes within a country or a group of countries	computers
health	space exploration
	a pop music band

    The European Union, or EU, was founded in 1957. At first, there were only six member states, including France, Italy, and West Germany. Nine other countries have joined since then. These countries have joined together partly because they want to avoid another catastrophe like World War II.

    In the future, the countries of the EU will develop greater economic, political, and social cooperation. Soon, many of the countries will be using the same currency — the euro. Within a few years, several more countries, such as Poland, Hungary, and the Czech Republic, will have joined the EU.

_____

_____

_____

_____

_____

_____

11 Life's little lessons

1 Milestones

A Read these statements. Are they true for you? Check (✓) True or False.
For statements that are false, write the true information.

	True	**False**
Example: As soon as I got my own telephone, I called all my friends.	☐	✓

The moment I got my own telephone, I called my parents.

or _I've never had my own telephone._

	True	False
1. By the time I was two years old, I had already learned two languages.	☐	☐
2. As soon as I got my driver's license, my parents let me drive everywhere.	☐	☐
3. Before I started school, I used to watch TV all day.	☐	☐
4. Once I started learning English, I quit studying other languages.	☐	☐
5. Until I went out on my first date, I was very shy.	☐	☐

B Write three true statements about yourself, your family, or your friends.

1. _____

2. _____

3. _____

2 **Complete these descriptions. Use words from the list.**

☐ ambitious	☐ carefree	☑ sophisticated
☐ argumentative	☐ generous	☐ tolerant

1. Kate is so _____sophisticated_____ . She always dresses well, she knows lots of famous people, and she never says anything silly.

2. I just spent a horrible evening with Gloria. She questioned and criticized everything I said. I wish she weren't so _____ .

3. My sister is very _____ . She never forgets her friends' birthdays and always gives them nice gifts.

4. Once I was sixteen years old, my parents became more _____ , and they let me do what I wanted.

5. Paul is really _____ . He wants to own his own business by the time he's 25.

6. I wish I could be like Debbie. She's so _____ and never seems to worry about anything.

3 **Do you have a best friend or some best friends? Write about one of them. In the first paragraph, describe the person. In the second paragraph, describe a particular time when the person helped you.**

> One of my best friends is Christine. She's very mature and sensible, and she always gives me good advice when I need it. Until I met her, I used to make some very bad decisions. . . .
>
> Christine is also very generous. She always gives her friends help when they need it. For example, the moment she found out I was sick last winter, she came and cooked dinner for me. She even . . . .

_____

_____

_____

_____

_____

_____

_____

4 *Turning points*

A Have you had any major turning points in your life? If so, what happened? If not, are there any major changes you would like to make?

NELSON MANDELA

Nelson Mandela was born in Transkei, South Africa, in 1918. He had an eventful life right from the beginning. While he was in high school, his father died, and he went to live with his cousin, David Dalindyebo. After he finished high school, he went to Fort Hare University College. In 1940, before he was able to graduate, Mandela was told to leave the college because he had taken part in a student strike. At about this same time, his family had chosen a girl for him to marry. Mandela wanted to choose his own wife, however, so he ran away from home and made his way to the city of Johannesburg.

Soon after Mandela moved to Johannesburg, he got a job as a policeman in a mine. Later, he began studying to be a lawyer. He also became involved in politics and joined the African National Congress, an organization that sought equality among all ethnic groups in South

Africa. At the same time, he studied for two university degrees. Then, in 1952, he and his friend, Oliver Tambo, opened the first black law firm in the country. During the next twelve years, Mandela practiced law, and was sent to prison several times for opposing the government's policy toward black South Africans.

Mandela's life changed completely in 1964 when a court found him guilty of trying to cause a revolution against the government. He was given "life imprisonment." During the next twenty-six years, Mandela became the world's most famous political prisoner. Mandela was finally released on February 9, 1990. Four years later, in the country's first free election, Mandela became the first black person to be elected President of South Africa.

B Read about some turning points in Nelson Mandela's life. Complete the chart with three turning points for each of the time periods.

Some turning points in Nelson Mandela's life	
1918–1940	*father died while he was still in high school*
1940–1964	
1964–1994	

5 *Regrets*

A Write sentences about each person's regret. Use *should (not) have*.

1. Eric was very argumentative with his boss, so she fired him.
   Eric shouldn't have been argumentative with his boss.

2. Marsha changed jobs. Now she works in a bank. Working in a large company is more interesting.

   _____

3. Ivan worked seven days a week for several years. Then he got very sick.

   _____

4. Carla refused every job offer she received. She's been unemployed for a year, and she no longer gets any job offers.

   _____

5. Andrew studied music in school, but he's much better at computer science.

   _____

6. Jim was completely carefree when he was a student, so he got very bad grades.

   _____

7. Francis spent too much money on her friends. Now she can't afford to take a vacation.

   _____

8. Judy was very naive when she was younger. She often lent money to "friends," but they never repaid her.

   _____

B Write about your own regrets. Write four sentences with *should (not) have*.

1. _____

2. _____

3. _____

4. _____

6 *If . . .*

A Rewrite the sentences using *if* clauses + past perfect and the words given.

1. I should have studied English sooner.

   If I'd studied English sooner, I would have gotten a better job.   (get a better job)

2. We should have made a reservation.

   _____   (eat already)

3. You should have let me drive.

   _____   (arrive by now)

4. I should have studied harder.

   _____   (pass my exams)

5. I should have been more sensible.

   _____   (save some money)

B Write sentences with *if* clauses. Use the words given and your own ideas.

1. argumentative *If I'd been less argumentative as a child,*
   I would have had a better relationship with my parents.

2. carefree _____

   _____

3. mature or immature _____

   _____

4. naive _____

   _____

5. rebellious _____

   _____

6. tolerant _____

   _____

7 *Complete the conversation. Circle the correct time expressions and use the correct tense of the verbs given.*

Andy: I've made such a mess of my life!

John: What do you mean?

Andy: If I ___hadn't accepted___ a job
(not accept)

(as soon as)/before/until) I graduated, I

_____
(travel)

around Europe all summer – just like you did.
You were so carefree.

John: You know, I should _____ to
(not go)

Europe. I should _____ the
(take)

great job I was offered. (After/Before/Until) I returned
from Europe, it was too late.

Andy: But my job's depressing! (Before/The moment/Until) I started it,
I hated it – on the very first day! That was two years ago, and nothing's
changed. I should _____ for another job right away.
(look)

John: Well, start looking now. There were some good jobs advertised on the Internet
last month. If I _____ the Internet,
(not check)

I _____ this great job listing.
(not see)

Andy: Really? What's the job?

John: It's working as a landscape gardener. (Before/The moment/Until)
I saw it, I knew it was right for me.

Andy: But for me right now, the problem is I get a very good salary, and I just
bought a house. If I _____ the house,
(not buy)

I _____ take a lower paying job.
(be able to)

John: Well, I guess you can't have everything. If I _____ a better salary,
(have)

I _____ a house, too.
(buy)

12 The right stuff

1 Complete these sentences with In order for *or* In order to.

1. *In order to* speak a foreign language well, it's a good idea to use the language as often as possible.

2. _____ a movie to be entertaining, it has to have good actors and an interesting story.

3. _____ succeed in business, you often have to work long hours.

4. _____ attract new members, a sports club needs to offer inexpensive memberships.

5. _____ a restaurant to be popular, it has to have attractive decor.

6. _____ a travel agency to succeed, it has to be able to find the cheapest airline tickets.

7. _____ make friends when you move to a new town, it's a good idea to join a club.

8. _____ a magazine to be successful, it needs to be well written and entertaining.

a successful magazine

2 Write sentences. Use the information in the box and In order to.

- ☐ hire talented salespeople
- ☐ think of a good gimmick
- ☑ keep up with your studies
- ☐ work extremely long hours
- ☐ provide excellent customer service

1. be a successful student

   In order to be a successful student, you have to keep up with your studies.

2. run a profitable clothes store

   _____

3. manage your own business

   _____

4. create a persuasive advertisement

   _____

5. run a successful automobile company

   _____

3 Choose the correct word or phrase.

1. I didn't enjoy this book on how to succeed in business. It wasn't very

   _____*well written*_____ . (poorly written/well typed/well written)

2. I learned a lot about how to run a successful bookstore from reading that magazine.

   I found it very _____ . (clever/entertaining/informative)

3. Linda has so many interesting ideas, and she's always thinking of new projects.

   She's very _____ . (dynamic/patient/tough)

4. Rosie is a salesperson, and she really knows how to do her job. She's so _____

   that she sells three times as much as her co-workers.   (friendly/good-looking/persuasive)

5. Daniel is one of the top models in the world. He works out at the gym every day so

   he looks really _____ . (athletic/risky/useful)

6. For a restaurant to succeed, it has to _____ a high level of

   quality in both food and service. (attract/keep up with/maintain)

7. If a department store improves its _____ and looks really attractive,

   it can attract a lot of new customers. (boutique/decor/safety record)

4 Read this information about journalists. Then write a paragraph about one of the people from the list or another person of your choice.

To be a successful journalist, you need to be both talented and dynamic. You have to write well and write quickly. In addition, you must be able to report a story accurately. Also, in order to report the news, a journalist needs to have a good knowledge of world and current events.

an artist	a homemaker	a manager/boss
a businessperson	a parent	a teacher

_____

_____

_____

_____

5 *A nice thing about it is . . . .*

A Look at the pictures. Describe two positive or negative features of each place. Use the words from the list or your own ideas.

1. shopping center

2. hotel

3. restaurant

4. disco

| ☐ attractive | ☑ crowded | ☐ dingy | ☐ old |
| ☑ clean | ☐ dancing | ☐ music | ☐ quiet |

1. A nice thing *about the shopping center is that it's clean.*
   Another nice thing *is that it's not too crowded.*

2. A bad thing _____
   Another bad thing _____

3. A good thing _____
   Another good thing _____

4. A great thing _____
   Another great thing _____

B Give two reasons why you like or dislike each place. Use your own ideas.

1. freeway

2. park

3. swimming pool

4. picnic area

1. I like the freeway *because it's not too crowded.*
   Also, I like it *because of the trees.*

2. The park is popular _____
   Also, I like it _____

3. I don't like the swimming pool _____
   Also, it's unpopular _____

4. The reason people go there _____
   I don't like it _____

6 *Use the words in the box to complete this crossword puzzle.*

advertising	megastore
athletic	new
calculated	persuasive
concepts	risky
dynamic	style
gimmick	talented
maintain	

Across

1 I was going to buy a cheap printer for my computer. However, the salesperson was very _____ , so I bought a more expensive one.

5 Our local Vietnamese restaurant has a great new _____ to encourage people to eat early – two dinners for the price of one if you arrive before 7:00!

7 Everything is brand-_____ and modern in the disco on First Street.

9 No one knows about Club Pacifico, so it's always empty.
It needs some really good _____ in the newspaper.

10 Charlie's Coffee Shop was just sold to a new owner. She has some interesting new ideas and _____ to improve it.

12 The jazz club has a great new band. They're supposed to be very _____ musicians.

13 My aunt took several _____ risks when she opened her boutique. Luckily, her ideas worked, and her shop is now much more successful.

Down

2 It's _____ to run a grocery store right next to a supermarket. Most people will probably think the supermarket is cheaper and buy all their food there.

3 The waitress at the Spanish restaurant is very _____ .
She works out at the gym and goes jogging every day.

4 For a taxi company to keep a good name, it has to _____ a very reliable service.

6 There's a _____ near my home. I can get everything I need there, so I never shop anywhere else!

8 Eva is a great flight attendant because she's really _____ .
In fact, she has more energy than anyone else I know.

11 Maybe I'm old-fashioned, but I don't like the latest _____ in clothes.

7 *Look at these advertisements and write two sentences about each one.*
Describe the features and give reasons why you like or dislike the advertisements.

Example: *A nice thing about the first ad is that it attracts your attention.*
I like it because of the clever concept.

1. _____

_____

2. _____

_____

3. _____

_____

8 *Success story*

A Think of a successful company. Why is it successful?

Success Stories

One of the most successful fashion companies in the world is Benetton. The Benetton family opened their first shop in Italy in 1968. Today, there are Benetton shops in major cities all over the world. Benetton followed four marketing principles in order to achieve their success.

The first principle is *Consumer Concept*. To build a successful business, you have to develop products around things people value, especially quality. The founder of Benetton began by asking people what they wanted. He created clothes to match people's wants: the style is casual; the colors and patterns are bold; and the quality is excellent.

The *Systems Link* is another feature of good marketing. For Benetton, this means waiting to get information about what customers like and what they dislike before making the clothes. In other words, Benetton's clothes are made to order.

The *Information Link* means making sure the company responds quickly to people's demands. When something is sold at a Benetton store, the store records information about the type, size, and color of the item. This information is then sent to the main office in Italy. Benetton can use this information to identify popular products and to continue making them; it can also identify less popular products and stop making them.

A final important marketing principle is the *Retail Link*. There are Benetton stores in countries around the world. All the stores have the same clothing, the same window displays, and the same approach to sales. This means that customers can go into any Benetton store in the world and be sure of what they are buying.

The things people like about Benetton stores are that the quality is always high and the prices are generally low. And that spells success.

UNITED COLORS OF BENETTON.

B Read the passage. Underline four reasons why Benetton is so successful.

C Can you think of two other stores that are run in a similar way to Benetton?

13 That's a possibility.

1

What do you think happened? Put the words in the correct order to make sentences.

A bus overturned on the freeway yesterday.

1. slippery been road have the might

   The road might have been slippery.

2. trouble the could engine bus had have

   _____

3. wheel off fallen a must have

   _____

4. fallen the have driver asleep may

   _____

The mayor didn't go to last night's fund-raiser.

5. have event forgotten couldn't she the

   She couldn't have forgotten the event.

6. she not come wanted have must to

   _____

7. the might she had time have not

   _____

8. not may she felt have well

   _____

2

What do you think happened? Write an explanation for each event using past modals.

1. *Someone might have broken into the house.*

2. _____

   _____

3. _____

   _____

4. _____

   _____

3 *Answer these questions. Write two explanations using past modals.*

Why do you think the ancient Britons built Stonehenge?

1. They might have _built it to use as a church._

2. _____

3. They could have _____

4. _____

How do you think early explorers communicated with people in the countries they visited?

What do you think happened in Roswell, New Mexico?

5. _____

6. _____

4 *Write two paragraphs about something strange that has happened to you. In the first paragraph, describe the situation. In the second paragraph, give two or three explanations for what happened.*

> I invited six friends to a barbecue on the beach. I suggested we meet at eight o'clock. They all said they would come and would bring some food.
> On the day of the barbecue, only two of my friends showed up. I guess my other friends could have overslept, or they might have decided to do something else. Another possibility is that they may have thought I meant 8 P.M. instead of 8 A.M. I'm not sure what happened!

_____

_____

_____

_____

_____

5 *The Abominable Snowman*

A In some countries, there are ancient stories about strange creatures similar to humans. For example, in Scandinavia, some people believe small creatures called elves live in the forests.

Are there any legends like this in your country? What are they?

He has been called the "missing link": half-man, half-beast. He is huge, maybe as much as 2.5 meters (about 8 feet) tall. His body is covered with long brown hair, but his face is hairless. His head is pointed, but he looks like a man. He walks upright, standing on two feet. He lives near the top of the highest mountain in the world – Mount Everest. He is known as the Abominable Snowman.

The legend of the Abominable Snowman is not new. For years, local people have reported seeing the creature they call "Yeti" – the all-eating animal – come down from the mountains and attack villagers. Climbers in the 1920s reported stories of huge footprints they saw high in the Himalayas – footprints unlike any animal's they had seen before.

In 1951, the explorer Eric Shipton took photographs of enormous tracks in the snow of Mount Everest. Shipton concluded that these footprints could not have been the tracks of any ordinary animal. He assumed that the Abominable Snowman really existed and must have walked around in that area.

These days, few people still believe in the Abominable Snowman. There have only been footprints in the snow as evidence of this creature. Scientists say there should have been more evidence. They suggest that the tracks may have been bear tracks. The sun can cause tracks to melt, and, when the tracks refreeze, they look like large footprints, such as those on Mount Everest.

If anyone ever succeeds in catching an Abominable Snowman, they may face a real problem: Would they put it in a zoo or give it a room in a hotel?

B Check (✓) True or False. For statements that are false, write the true information.

	True	False
1. The Abominable Snowman was first seen by climbers in the 1920s.	☐	☐
2. Scientists have captured one of the Yetis.	☐	☐
3. In 1951, Shipton took photographs of a Yeti.	☐	☐
4. Most scientists believe Yetis really exist.	☐	☐

6 *Should have, could have, would have*

A What should or shouldn't these people have done?
Read each situation and check (✓) the best suggestion.

1. Joe's old car broke down on the highway. He left the
   car on the side of the road and walked home.
   ☐ He should have waved down a passing
      car for help.
   ☐ He shouldn't have left his car on the
      side of the road.
   ☐ He should have walked to a pay phone
      and called a tow truck.

2. Linda was in a park. She saw some people
   leave all their trash after they had finished
   their picnic. She did nothing.
   ☐ She did the right thing.
   ☐ She should have told them to throw
      away their trash.
   ☐ She could have thrown away the trash herself.

3. John saw a three-year-old child walking alone
   in a shopping mall. He took the child home
   and immediately called the police.
   ☐ He shouldn't have taken the child home.
   ☐ He should have left the child alone.
   ☐ He could have waited with the child until
      the parents returned.

4. Mrs. Judd wouldn't let her children watch TV for a month
   because they broke a window playing baseball.
   ☐ She could have made them pay for the window.
   ☐ She shouldn't have done anything. It was an accident.
   ☐ She shouldn't have let them play baseball for a month.

5. Martha's boss borrowed $20 from her a month ago but he forgot
   to pay her back. Martha never said anything about it.
   ☐ She should have demanded her money back.
   ☐ She shouldn't have loaned it to him.
   ☐ She could have written him a note asking for the money.

B What would you have done in the situations in part A?
Write suggestions or comments using past modals.

1. *I would have called a friend to give me a ride home.*
2. _____
3. _____
4. _____
5. _____

7 Nouns and verbs

A Complete the chart.

Noun	Verb	Noun	Verb
advice	*advise*	excuse	_____
_____	assume	_____	predict
conclusion	_____	suggestion	_____
_____	criticize	_____	warn

B Complete the sentences using words from the chart in part A. For the verbs, use *shouldn't have* + past participle. For the nouns, use the appropriate singular or plural form.

1. Josh __*shouldn't have criticized*__ me for wearing jeans and a T-shirt to a friend's party.

2. Millie told me she wasn't married, so I thought she was single. I shouldn't have jumped to _____ . Later, I found out that she was engaged to Joel.

3. Justin _____ having a beach party. It was so cold that we all got sick.

4. Phil _____ I would still be awake at midnight. I was asleep when he called.

5. Jill said she was late because she got caught in traffic. Hmm! I've heard that _____ before.

6. The weather report said it would rain today. Someone must have forgotten to look outside! That _____ was completely wrong. It's been sunny all day.

7. My professor _____ me to take a course in English literature. I have absolutely no interest in it.

8. I'll give you just this one _____ , but don't you ever ride my motorcycle without my permission again.

8 *Complete these conversations. Use past modals in the box and the verbs given. (More than one modal is possible.)*

could have
may have
might have
must have
should have

1. A: Where's Alex? He's late.

   B: He ___*may have gotten*___ (get) stuck in rush-hour traffic.

   A: He's always late! You know, he ___*should have bought*___ (buy) a cell phone last month when there was that great sale. Then he could tell us what the problem is.

2. A: Nina never responded to my invitation.

   B: She _____ (not receive) it.

   You _____ (call) her.

3. A: Jeff hasn't answered his phone for a week.

   B: He _____ (go) on vacation.

   He _____ (tell) you, though – sometimes he's very inconsiderate.

4. A: I can never fax Susan. There was something wrong with her machine again this morning.

   B: Yeah, I have the same problem faxing her. Her machine

   _____ (run out) of paper. She

   _____ (check) the machine.

5. A: Martin is strange. Sometimes he works really hard, but sometimes he seems pretty lazy. Last week, he hardly did any work.

   B: Well, you know, he _____ (not feel) well.

   Still, he _____ (tell) you that he was sick.

6. A: I ordered a book a month ago, but the store still hasn't called me back to say the book has arrived.

   B: They _____ (have) a problem with the

   publisher, but they _____ (let) you know.

14 Behind the scenes

1 *Complete the conversation. Use the passive form of the verbs given.*

Vera: Putting on a fashion show must be really challenging, Isaac.

Isaac: Yeah, but it's also fun. All the clothes have to ___be numbered___ (number)

so that the models wear them in the right sequence. And they also have to

_____ (mark) with the name of the right model.

Vera: What happens if something _____ (wear) by the wrong model?

Isaac: Well, naturally, it looks terrible! First impressions are the most important. A lot of

designer clothes _____ (sell) because they look good at the show.

Vera: Do you have to rehearse for a fashion show?

Isaac: Of course! They're more than just models and clothes.

Special lighting _____ (use), and almost always

music _____ (play) during the show.

Vera: It sounds complicated.

Isaac: Oh, it is. And at some fashion shows, a commentary may _____ (give).

Vera: A commentary? What do you mean?

Isaac: Well, someone talks about the clothes as they _____ (show)

on the runway by the models.

Vera: It sounds like timing is really important.

Isaac: Exactly. Everything has to _____ (time) perfectly,

otherwise the show may _____ (spoil).

2 Complete this passage. Use the passive form of the verbs given.

1. Nowadays, all sorts of things ___*are produced*___ (produce) in factories, including lettuce! At one food factory, fresh green lettuce _____ (grow) without sunlight or soil. Here is how it _____ (do).

2. Lettuce seedlings _____ (place) at one end of a long production line. Conveyor belts _____ (use) to move the seedlings slowly along. The tiny plants _____ (expose) to light from fluorescent lamps.

3. They have to _____ (feed) through the roots with plant food and water that _____ (control) by a computer.

4. Thirty days later, the plants _____ (collect) at the other end of the conveyor belts.

5. They may _____ (deliver) to the vegetable market the same day.

3 Choose the correct words or phrases.

1. Often, special music has to be _____ for a film.
   (composed/designed/hired)

2. A play may be _____ for several weeks before it is shown to the public.
   (shot/taken/rehearsed)

3. Designing _____ for actors to wear requires a lot of creativity.
   (scripts/sets/costumes)

4. Newspapers are _____ to stores after they are printed.
   (expanded/distributed/reported)

5. _____ are added after the film has been put together.
   (Sound effects/Special effects/Takes)

4 *International Puppets*

A Have you ever seen a puppet show? What was it like? Did you enjoy it?

International Puppets

The first puppets are thought to have been used in India over 4,000 years ago – probably even before actors. Since then, different kinds of puppets have become popular around the world.

Hand puppets are usually about 50 cm (20 inches) tall. Their main feature is a large head that has a costume with arms attached to it. These puppets are worn like a glove. The puppeteer, who stands below the stage, operates the puppet with his or her fingers. Hand puppets are widely used in European countries, such as Italy, France, and Britain.

Rod puppets have long been used in Japan and Italy and are now very popular in Eastern Europe. They are similar in shape to hand puppets but are much bigger – sometimes over 1 meter (40 inches) tall. The puppeteer, who works from below the stage, operates the puppet with rods that are attached to it: a thick rod fixed to the puppet's back, and thinner rods fixed to its neck, head, and arms. The puppeteer, holding the thick rod in one hand and the thinner rods in the other hand, can move the parts separately.

Shadow puppets are constructed in a similar way to rod puppets but are unique in that they are flat and much smaller – about 50 cm (20 inches). In addition, they are seen by audiences in a completely different way – these puppets appear as shadows on a screen that is lighted from behind. They are controlled either from below or beside the stage. Shadow puppets, which originally came from China, Java, and Indonesia, later became popular in Turkey and Greece.

Marionettes are puppets that are constructed from several small parts. Their height varies, and they are

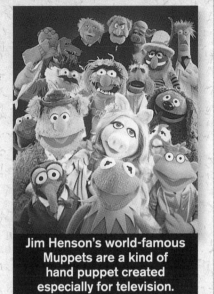

Jim Henson's world-famous Muppets are a kind of hand puppet created especially for television.

moved by strings that are usually controlled from above. Many marionettes are hung on nine strings, but there are some in Myanmar (formerly Burma) that have up to sixty strings. They can be made to perform interesting tricks, such as blowing smoke from a pipe.

B Complete the chart.

	Hand puppets	Rod puppets	Shadow puppets	Marionettes
Size				
How constructed?				
How moved?				
Position of puppeteer				
Where commonly used				

5 *Join these sentences with <u>who</u> or <u>that</u>. Add commas (,) wherever needed.*

journalists

the actors and actress from "Seinfeld"

Examples:

Foreign correspondents are journalists.
They report on one part of the world.

Foreign correspondents are journalists that report on one part of the world.

A newspaper reporter has to do a lot of research on news stories.
He or she is often new to journalism.

A newspaper reporter, who is often new to journalism, has to do a lot of research on news stories.

1. A movie director creates the film you see on the screen.
   He or she is often hired after the script is written.

   _____

   _____

2. A magician is a talented entertainer.
   He or she has to be good at creating illusions.

   _____

   _____

3. An on-call technician is a skilled person.
   He or she responds to calls from people with computer problems.

   _____

   _____

4. Fashion models have to make designer clothes look good.
   They are almost always young and good-looking.

   _____

   _____

5. TV sitcoms include actors and actresses.
   They are recognized by television viewers around the world.

   _____

   _____

6 Match the definitions with the jobs.

1. a film editor __c__

    a. a journalist who specializes in reporting on the personal lives of famous people

2. a gossip columnist _____

    b. someone who looks for new people to work as actors or models

3. a graphic designer _____

    ✓ c. someone that helps a movie director put together the best "takes"

4. a stagehand _____

    d. a person who does dangerous scenes in a movie in the place of an actor

5. a stunt person _____

    e. a TV personality who invites guests to come on his or her program

6. a sportswriter _____

    f. a person who moves sets and furniture for theater and film productions

7. a talent scout _____

    g. a journalist who reports on sporting events such as football and tennis

8. a talk show host _____

    h. someone that creates the design for a printed work

7 Choose one of the jobs in Exercise 6 or another job to write about. In the first paragraph, describe which job you would like to have and why. In the second paragraph, describe what the job involves behind the scenes. Use relative clauses in some of your descriptions.

If I worked in TV, I'd like to be a talk show host like Oprah Winfrey. A talk show host, who is responsible for choosing guests for the program, gets to meet and talk to people with different interests and problems. I would enjoy facing serious issues head on and dealing with them. . . .

Behind the scenes, a TV talk show host is the person that works with a team of researchers to think of the topics to discuss on the program. Then, he or she also helps write the interview questions for the show. The host is also the person who finds experts to advise guests on how to deal with their problems. . . .

8 **Describe six steps in the process of building a house. Use the words given in the boxes. Use the passive form of the verbs.**

1. architect

4. plumber

2. builders

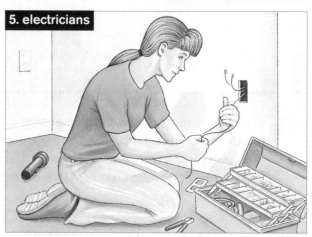

5. electricians

3. carpenters

6. painters

1. First, *the house is designed by an architect.* (design)
2. Next, _____ (construct)
3. Then _____ (make)
4. After that, _____ (fit)
5. Then _____ (put in)
6. Finally, _____ (paint)

84

15 There should be a law!

1 *What should be done about each situation? Write sentences about these pictures. Use the passive form with <u>should</u>, <u>shouldn't</u>, or <u>ought to</u>.*

Leaving trash in the streets

Playing car stereos late at night

Writing graffiti on walls

Not maintaining public transportation well

1. *People shouldn't be allowed to leave trash in the streets.*

or *People ought to be required to pick up their own trash.*

2. _____

_____

3. _____

_____

4. _____

_____

85

2

Write sentences about these pictures. Use the passive form with <u>have to</u>, <u>must</u>, *or* <u>mustn't</u>.

1. <u>*A law has to be passed to prevent people from losing their homes.*</u>

or <u>*Something must be done to repair abandoned homes.*</u>

2. _____

_____

3. _____

_____

4. _____

_____

3 *Respond to these opinions. Use suitable expressions from the box and then give your own opinion.*

> I agree/disagree with you because . . . .
> That's not a bad idea. On the other hand, I feel . . . .
> You may have a point. Nevertheless, I think . . . .
> In my opinion, ...
> Do you? I don't think . . . .

1. A: Chinese is a very useful language to learn.
   B: *I agree with you because there are millions*
      of Chinese-speaking people.

2. A: I think having a pet makes you more relaxed.
   B: _____

3. A: Public transportation should be provided free of charge.
   B: _____

4. A: I think having a car is almost a necessity nowadays.
   B: _____

5. A: In my opinion, all plastic containers should be banned.
   B: _____

4 *Think of four things that you have strong opinions about. Write your opinions and explain your reasons for them. Use passive modals.*

Example: *In my opinion, a four-day week should be given to everyone*
         because people need more free time.

1. I feel that _____

2. I think that _____

3. In my opinion, _____

4. I don't think that _____

5 *Taking the law into your own hands*

A Have you ever been so annoyed with your neighbors that you did something to annoy them in return? If so, what did your neighbors do to annoy you? What did you do in return?

In my apartment building, there is one parking space for each apartment. If a family has two cars, the second car has to be parked on the street. There was no problem until I worked out of town for a month. When I came back, my neighbors Erica and Chris had parked their second car in my space. I asked them to move it, but they refused. They said, "In our opinion, you don't really need a parking space because you go away so often."

The apartment manager said the problem had to be settled among ourselves. When Erica and Chris went on vacation, I bought an old clunker car and parked it in their space.

My neighbors used to keep rabbits in their yard, but they treated them very badly. Rabbits should be cleaned regularly, but these rabbits were very dirty, and the smell was really terrible. Worse, I noticed that the rabbits didn't have enough to eat or drink. When I complained to my neighbors, they said, "We don't think it's any of your business. They're not your rabbits, are they?"

When I called the animal protection society, they said they would investigate. I waited a week, but nothing happened. One night, I stole the rabbits and took them home. The next day I gave them to a local pet store.

I hadn't been able to get any sleep because of a dripping noise coming from my air conditioner. I thought the air conditioner needed to be repaired, so I called a technician. She couldn't find anything wrong with it, but she said she thought the dripping was coming from the air conditioner in the apartment above me. I asked the neighbor who lives above me to have his air conditioner checked, but he said, "If you can't sleep, that's your problem!"

The following day, I went up a ladder and attached a plastic pipe to my neighbor's leaking air conditioner. Then I stuck the pipe through my neighbor's bedroom window. The next night, my neighbor's bedroom was flooded!

B Complete the chart.

Problem	First attempts to solve it	Final solution
1.		
2.		
3.		

6 *Add tag questions to these statements.*

> **Grammar note:** Tag questions
>
> With most verbs in the simple present tense, use *do, does, don't,* or *doesn't* to make tag questions.
>
> Groceries cost a lot these days, **don't** they?
> Health insurance doesn't cover all medical problems, **does** it?

1. It isn't easy to make ends meet these days, ____*is it*____ ?
2. The city doesn't provide enough services for elderly people, ____*does it*____ ?
3. You can easily spend all your money on food and rent, _____ ?
4. Some unemployed people don't really want to work, _____ ?
5. Car insurance is getting more and more expensive, _____ ?
6. There are a lot of homeless people, _____ ?
7. Some companies have excellent day-care services, _____ ?
8. Laws should be passed to reduce street crime, _____ ?

7 *Nouns and verbs*

A Complete the chart.

Noun	Verb	Noun	Verb
abolition	abolish	gambling	_____
abuse	_____	_____	improve
_____	advertise	insurance	_____
consumption	_____	_____	provide
_____	disturb	requirement	_____

B Write four sentences with tag questions using words from the chart. Use two of the nouns and two of the verbs.

Example: *The practice of keeping animals in cages*
should be abolished, shouldn't it?

1. _____
   _____
2. _____
3. _____
4. _____

8 *Give one reason for and one reason against these opinions.*

1. Children should be made to study a foreign language in primary school.

   For: *It would help children understand other cultures.*

   Against: *I don't think it would be easy to find enough teachers.*

2. Battery-operated cars should be developed by auto companies.

   For: _____

   Against: _____

3. Much more tax money ought to be spent on improving health-care services.

   For: _____

   Against: _____

4. Public transportation should be provided free of charge, shouldn't it?

   For: _____

   Against: _____

9 *Complete the conversation. Use passive modals and tag questions.*

Tony: Scientists should _____ to do

     medical research.   (make)

Kate: Why do you say that?

Tony: Well, good health is the most valuable thing

     in life, _____ ?

Kate: You may have a point. Nevertheless, I feel

     that researchers ought _____

     to study whatever they choose.   (allow)

Tony: But some subjects aren't very

     important, _____ ?

Kate: Oh, Tony, you can't really deny the

     importance of other subjects, _____ ?

Tony: Like what?

Kate: Well, what about research into different ways

     of producing more food? That should be a

     priority, too, _____ ?

Tony: Oh, I guess you're right, Kate.

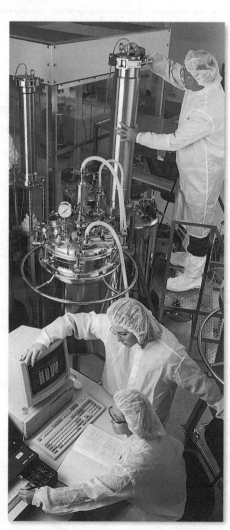

16 Challenges and accomplishments

1 *The best and the worst of it*

A Complete the chart with ideas of your own.

Job	One of the best things	One of the worst things
1. social worker	*helping people*	
2. running your own business		*being responsible for everything*
3. dentist	*earning good money*	
4. doctor in a hospital		*working long hours*
5. farmer	*getting lots of fresh air*	
6. using a computer all day		*getting eye strain*
7. working with young children	*seeing kids learn about life*	
8. builder		*working outside in bad weather*

B Write about the positive and negative aspects of the jobs in part A.

1. *One of the best things about being a social worker is helping people.*
   One of the worst things is _____

2. _____

3. _____

4. _____

5. _____

6. _____

7. _____

8. _____

2 *Choose the correct word.*

1. The thing I like most about being a dog trainer is
   giving dogs a _____ when they
   follow commands.   (relaxation/relief/reward)

2. A difficult thing about being a songwriter is making
   sure your songs are a _____ .
   If a song is unpopular, you just don't earn
   any money.   (failure/punishment/success)

3. Some people get really scared about flying. As a
   flight attendant, you have to deal with passengers'
   _____ .   (anxiety/aspects/joy)

4. A great thing about being a nurse is getting lots
   of _____ . People are always telling
   us how well we do our work.   (criticism/praise/sadness)

3 *Complete the sentences with information about the jobs in the box.*

acting in movies	being unemployed	✓teaching young children
being a student	doing volunteer work	writing for a magazine

1. One of the most rewarding aspects *of teaching young children is seeing them develop so quickly.*

2. The most challenging thing _____

3. One of the rewards _____

4. One of the most difficult things _____

5. The most interesting aspect _____

6. One of the least interesting aspects _____

4 *Write two paragraphs about a job you find interesting. In the first paragraph, describe some positive aspects of the job. In the second paragraph, describe some of its negative aspects.*

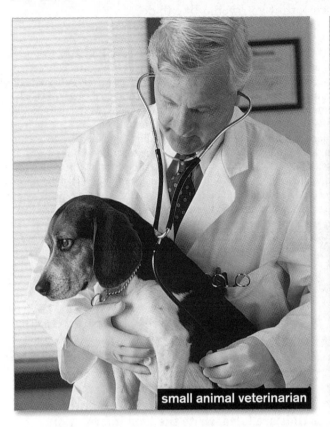

small animal veterinarian

large animal veterinarian

Being a veterinarian is both rewarding and challenging. People bring animals with different sorts of problems into the clinic every day. One of the best things about the job is treating and curing those animals that are seriously sick or injured. It's an amazing thing to be able to save an animal and bring a smile to a pet owner's face.

Sometimes, if an animal is very sick or badly injured, it's not possible to treat it successfully. The saddest aspect of the job is dealing with animals you cannot save. It's a considerable loss for both the vet and the pet owner.

5   *Huge challenges, enormous rewards*

A   Have you ever done volunteer work? If so, what kind of work did you do? If not, is there any kind of volunteer work that you would like to do?

Médecins Sans Frontières (MSF), which means "Doctors Without Borders," was established in 1971. It is now the world's largest independent organization that provides emergency medical relief. The aim of the organization is to help people who have suffered badly in wars or natural disasters, such as earthquakes or floods.

Each year, about 3,000 people are sent abroad to work in over seventy different countries worldwide. MSF relies on volunteer professionals but also works closely with local professionals; in most projects, there are seven local staff members to every one foreigner. Volunteers are paid about $800 a month and receive travel expenses. They usually work for nine months to a year on a project and then go home; however, about 50% of volunteers go on more than

one mission. One volunteer reports, "Working in politically sensitive areas with limited resources can be frustrating, but there is huge satisfaction in making even a small or temporary difference to people. What better recommendation than to say I'm about to leave on a third mission!"

What qualities and skills do you need to become a volunteer? You have to be able to deal with stress, and you

need to be able to work independently as well as in a team. You are not required, however, to have medical qualifications. Besides medical professionals, MSF needs the skilled support of technical staff such as building engineers and food experts.

The reaction of volunteers returning from MSF speaks for itself. "One of my biggest challenges was organizing a team to open a new hospital in a town that had had no medical care for three years," one volunteer said. This volunteer concluded that the project was a success for two reasons: the reduction of deaths and the fact that the local people were so thankful. Another volunteer says, "With MSF, I have had the chance to travel and test my skills to the limits both professionally and personally. The rewards can be enormous."

B   Check (✓) True or False. For statements that are false, write the true information.

	True	False
1. Médecins Sans Frontières provides worldwide emergency medical relief.	☐	☐
2. There are more local people than foreigners working on most MSF projects.	☐	☐
3. Most volunteers work on only one project.	☐	☐
4. You have to be a medical professional to volunteer for MSF.	☐	☐

C   What are two challenges the volunteers mention in the article? What are two rewards?

Challenges	Rewards

6 **Choose the correct prepositions.**

□ about	□ by	□ for	✔ from	□ in	□ of

1. In the next few years, I'd like to have lived in a culture that's very
   different __*from*__ my own.
2. For me, the most difficult aspect _____ working abroad is learning
   a foreign language.
3. I'd like to have gotten another degree _____ two years.
4. Working _____ an organization like the Peace Corps is very rewarding.
5. I hope I'll have gotten married _____ the time
   I'm thirty.
6. One of the most exciting things _____ working
   abroad is learning about another culture.

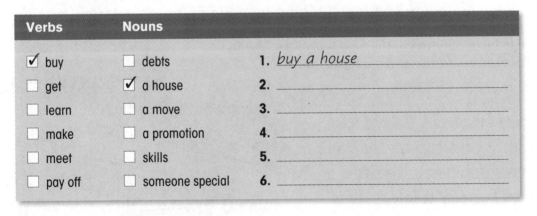
working abroad

7 **Collocations**

A Match the verbs with the nouns. Write the
collocations. (More than one answer may be possible.)

Verbs	Nouns	
✔ buy	□ debts	1. *buy a house*
□ get	✔ a house	2. _____
□ learn	□ a move	3. _____
□ make	□ a promotion	4. _____
□ meet	□ skills	5. _____
□ pay off	□ someone special	6. _____

B Write a sentence with each collocation. Use the present perfect,
past simple, future perfect, or *would like to have* + past participle.

1. *Alex and Mariko have managed to buy a house.*
   I expect to have bought a house within five years.
2. _____
3. _____
4. _____
5. _____
6. _____

8 Personal portraits

A Write three sentences about the accomplishments of someone you know very well. Use the present perfect or simple past.

Example:

By carefully investing his money, my friend Paulo has been able to retire at 30. He has managed to set up an organization that helps find jobs for people who are homeless. In addition, he . . . .

_____

_____

_____

_____

_____

B Write three sentences about things the same person would like to have achieved in the next ten years. Use the future perfect or *would like to have* + past participle.

Example:

Paulo would like to have traveled a lot by the time he's 40. He hopes to have started an organization to provide scholarships for needy college students. He also hopes he'll have . . . .

_____

_____

_____

_____

_____